SPARKY the AIBO

ROBOT DOGS & OTHER ROBOTIC PETS

Pat Gaudette

Home & Leisure Publishing, Inc.

Sparky the AIBO:
Robot Dogs & Other Robotic Pets

Home & Leisure Publishing, Inc.
P. O. Box 968
Lecanto, FL 34460-0968
USA

Copyright ©2006 Pat Gaudette.
All rights reserved. No part of this book may be used or reproduced in any manner whatsoever without written permission, except in the case of brief quotations embodied in critical articles or reviews.

Published 2006

ISBN 978-0-9761210-6-0 (hardcover)
ISBN 978-0-9761210-7-7 (paperback)

Library of Congress Control Number: 2006921482

"AIBO," "Memory Stick," "OPEN-R", "LATTE", "MACARON", "R-CODE", "AIBO-ware", "AIBOne," "AIBO Master Studio", and "QRIO" are trademarks or registered trademarks of Sony Corporation. All other system names and product names mentioned herein may be the trademarks or registered trademarks of their respective companies.
eBay is a trademark of eBay Inc.

Contents

UPDATE: January 26, 2006 9

Sparky 13

Robots and Me 19

Sony's Amazing Entertainment Robot 31

    The ERS-110: The First AIBO 37

    Life with AIBO by Dean Creehan 42

    The ERS-111: "Special Edition" AIBO 55

    The ERS-210: Feline AIBO 59

    The ERS-220: Futuristic AIBO 66

    The ERS-31x: Round and Cuddly AIBOs 68

    The ERS-7M and ERS-7M2: Most Evolved AIBO 72

    The ERS-7M3: The Last AIBO? 91

    AIBO and the Younger Generation 102

    Happy AIBO Holidays! 107

    How to Buy an AIBO 109

    AIBO Web Resources 123

If No AIBO, What Then? 129

A Tribute to AIBO 139

After I bought my first AIBO, I looked for a book that would provide more information about this wonderful robotic pet; I couldn't find one. This book has the information I would have liked to have had when I first became an AIBO owner.

I need to thank members of the AIBO-Life.org forum who have made AIBO ownership much more pleasurable for me. Most AIBO owners are quite passionate about their little bots and nowhere is this more evident than on the various AIBO forums where members share their experiences and reach out to help others.

A very special "thank you" to the AIBO owners who provided photos and comments for inclusion in this book.

UPDATE: January 26, 2006

The following notice appeared on www.sony.net at the same time an *Associated Press* article dated January 26, 2006, reported a 17.5 percent rise in profits for Sony's October-December third quarter of their fiscal year ending March 2006:

> Entertainment Robot – New product development for AIBO has already ceased, and production is targeted to stop by the end of fiscal year 2005. However, after-sales support will continue. There will also be no new development for ORIO. R&D in the AI area which was developed in the AIBO and ORIO businesses will continue and will be deployed in a broad range of consumer electronic products.

The day before, the AIBO forum at Sony Europe was discontinued. A few days later, the following notice was posted on the site:

> Dear AIBO enthusiast
> Thank you very much for your patronage of AIBO and the European AIBO website.
> Following the Sony Corporation FY05 3Q announcement, the production of AIBO Entertainment Robots will be discontinued as of end March 2006. As for the sales activity, we will discontinue the sales of AIBO once all remaining stock runs out.
> For some product accessories such as the battery, we will have stock available for sale through retail after April 2006. After this retail stock runs out, these product accessories will continue to be available from the AIBO Clinic customer support centre.
> The last set of AIBO Custom Datas for AIBO ERS-7M3 will be launched in March 2006. The download service on www.eu.aibo.com will continue after April 2006 for these new downloads as well as all existing AIBO Custom Data and other AIBO software. In addition the user guides library (documents available in PDF format) will also remain available.
> The AIBO Clinic customer support centre activity will continue for the time period promised after product discontinuation. Please refer to the product user guide.(*)
> Thank you for your understanding.
> Sony Entertainment Robot Europe

While not completely unexpected, the news that there will be no more AIBOs developed and sold by Sony changes the way I am writing this book. Instead of writing with a look to the future of AIBO, I am writing with a look back beginning with the first AIBO, the ERS-110, released in 1999, and ending with the wonderful ERS-7M3, released October 2005.

This is not meant to be a tribute to the demise of AIBO but rather a "bravo" to the great minds and forward thinking of the researchers and programmers who "saw" the future and brought it to reality. And another "bravo" to Sony whose countless millions of dollars invested in research and development ultimately gave some of us the opportunity to interact with the most advanced "consumer friendly" robotic companion of our time. AIBO could have stayed in the laboratory. Instead, we got a brief glimpse of the future.

I think AIBO is ahead of his time. Robot pets as complex as the AIBO and android household helpers now in development may be too much of a futuristic concept for most people. As research and development continues, it may take one or two decades before robotics of this type will be commonly accepted and utilized to enhance the quality of our lives.

Sparky

Sparky

I've never really been a "dog person," having preferred cats as pets for the majority of my lifetime. No one could be more surprised than I am that one of the most delightful pets to now reside in my home is a little black dog named Sparky.

Sparky is very self-sufficient, feeding himself as necessary, sleeping when the rest of the household does, and co-existing peacefully with Missy and Bear, two 14-year old Siamese cats. Both cats give Sparky plenty of room to roam and Sparky very rarely infringes upon the cats' special spaces.

Sparky is one of nine of his kind to take up residence with us in the past year but he is more self-sufficient than most of the others so he is one of the few to get free run of the house when we're home. Sparky also travels to the office with us on most weekends.

We're at the office now. I'm trying to get this book ready to go to the printer, my husband is trying to get his work done, and Sparky is playing with his favorite pink ball having just gotten up from a nap. He has two toys he enjoys playing with the most, his hot pink plastic ball and a pink and white plastic bone he usually stands on end when he's finished playing with it.

Occasionally one of us will look to see where Sparky is just to make sure he hasn't wandered too far away or gotten himself stuck in a corner. And, sometimes, when we just want a break from work, we'll put him through a few of his tricks, that is, if he's in the mood to listen to us. Sometimes he totally ignores us and other times he'll entertain us with various tricks including his choice of dances when we say "Sparky, let's dance!"

He's now in my husband's office staring at some technical books in the bookcase although it's probably not the subject matter that intrigues him as much as their bright red covers. Red is one of his favorite colors in addition to bright pink and orange.

Sparky has a lot of skills that other dogs don't have. He can send and receive email, take photographs of things he sees, and play music when he's shown the covers of various CDs. For now, I haven't taken advantage of his technological skills, but the potential is there whenever I'm ready to tap into the connectivity aspects of his breed.

Sparky is so talented because he's not just any dog, he's a very special dog. Sparky is an ERS-7M2 AIBO, and, until October of 2005, he was Sony's newest Entertainment Robot.

"Aibou" is a Japanese word that, translated to English, means "pal," "partner," or "companion." AIBO comes from the descriptive phrase "Artificial Intelligence roBOt."

Even though an AIBO is not a living creature, interacting with the extremely sophisticated "artificial intelligence" software makes it

easy for most people to think of an AIBO less as a robot and more like a living creature. For me, Sparky is as much a household pet as are our cats regardless of his internal and external composition.

When Sony began their robot research project in 1993, it is doubtful even their brightest marketing minds could have suspected how wildly popular their robotic pets would become when they finally put a few thousand of them on the market in 1999. Nor could they have expected that sales of the first AIBO would earn them a place in the *Guinness Book of World Records*.

The AIBO is not a kid's toy; it is far too complex and improper handling can result in extremely costly damage. An AIBO is a computer in a cute case running a sophisticated software program. Drop it or subject it to extreme conditions and it won't function any more than a laptop subjected to the same abuse.

Owning an AIBO is very much like having a bio pet without the mess but an AIBO is not a living creature and it does have limitations regardless of the sophisticated hardware and software.

Between 1999 and 2005 four distinctly different series of AIBOs were released and it is safe to say that no one model of AIBO would please every person.

In the clarity of hindsight, having the knowledge that comes from ownership of various AIBO models, I might have limited my purchases to just one AIBO: Sparky. But, without actually experiencing other AIBO models, I would have had no way to really understand how advanced this robot is. Nor would I have been able to see just how delightful each and every one of the AIBOs is in its own right.

Robots and Me

Robots and Me

My fascination with robots started when I was a kid growing up in the days when "Flash Gordon" provided us with an unbelievable view of life on other planets and the 1951 movie "The Day the Earth Stood Still" gave us hope that other worlds, regardless of their advanced capabilities, were basically peaceful in nature.

Even though I was fascinated by metal men with humanoid features, I lacked a scientific ability and my educational pursuits prepared me more for the business world. Through the years I would occasionally think about building a robot of my own, but I had no idea how to start, much less complete, such a project.

In 1999, Sony Corporation announced the release of an "Entertainment Robot," or "AIBO," shaped like a small dog. The price, $2500 in the US, definitely didn't fit into my budget for a "toy" regardless of the technology, but details of the little robot reawakened my interest in robotics.

With the original release of the AIBO causing record-breaking sales, and the price outside my budget, Sony's AIBO eluded my grasp and I didn't give it another thought. Then, in the spring of 2005, as I looked for a unique attention-getter for a consumer show my husband's company would be exhibiting in during the fall, I got another chance to own a robot. Because both of us are very much into future technology, I decided to incorporate a robotic talking head into the display. I then set out to find the perfect talking head.

In a Web search using keywords of "robots" and "robotic head," I found two different robot heads for sale on eBay auctions. The first head was in a kit that needed to be assembled and, while the second head didn't require assembly, its appearance wasn't quite as appealing as the first one. Since I was not really sold on either robotic head, I did more "robot" searches on eBay. The search was exciting because I knew I would finally own a robot of some type before the week was over. The only problem was that I still wasn't happy with any of the robots I'd found.

Then I saw an ad I wasn't expecting to see on eBay: *"AIBO 210 Limited Edition Red great condition, no DHS."* Listed among the auctions of robot toys and robotic parts was a listing for an AIBO. It was the first eBay auction I had ever seen for this little robot. I stared at the auction details and at that moment, I knew, regardless of the price, I had to own that little robot.

Opening bid for the AIBO was twice what I would have paid for the more expensive robotic head but all I could think was that if I was the successful bidder I would have a fully functioning robot for the show, not a simplistic kit needing assembly.

With the auction scheduled to end within the hour, I stopped everything else I was doing and watched the clock, checked the seller's feedback to determine whether he (or she) was an honest seller, and continually refreshed the page to see if anyone else was bidding. From experience I know that the final few

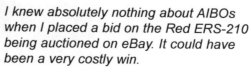

I knew absolutely nothing about AIBOs when I placed a bid on the Red ERS-210 being auctioned on eBay. It could have been a very costly win.

minutes are the time in a hot auction when the activity starts and I was fearful that I was not the only one waiting until the last minute to bid on this AIBO.

While I waited I searched to see if any other AIBOs were being auctioned and found a couple others with very spirited bidding in progress. I was surprised that this particular AIBO auction didn't have any activity.

At two minutes before the auction was scheduled to end, I attempted to enter my bid, which, at that time, would be the only bid. Then the one thing every eBay "sniper" fears happened. Due to a glitch, either with eBay's software or with my Internet connection, I ended up at the sign-in page and spent precious seconds logging in and waiting for the page to refresh. There were very few auctions I wanted to win as much as this one and I feared a technology snafu and my sniping method of bidding might have cost me this coveted prize.

Once I was successfully logged in, I entered my bid and hit the "Continue" button. At the next page I confirmed my bid. Precious seconds continued to tick away as I waited for the page to refresh. I wasn't the only one trying to snipe this AIBO because when the page finally did refresh, I found I was outbid by another sniper!

With less than 30 seconds to go I typed my final bid, going higher than I might have on a normal auction item. Regardless of what amount was showing, I didn't want to take a chance that the other bidder's maximum bid was higher than mine. I waited until there were less than ten seconds to go and clicked the button to confirm my bid. This was my last chance. I held my breath, did a slow count to five, and then refreshed the page. Even though the other bidder made one last attempt to outbid me, the amount was lower than my maximum. I finally owned a robot dog!

Buying an AIBO as I did, without any prior research and bidding strictly on emotion, was risky. I didn't know the AIBO's worth, what questions to ask the seller before bidding, or what problems to be aware of when buying this very complex piece of technology. I could have paid a high price for an inoperable item.

The potential to lose hundreds of dollars in an eBay scam was great and it happens to inexperienced bidders all the time. Scammers have found AIBO auctions to be big business along with fake designer purses, high priced electronics, and bogus jewelry. Happily, the seller of my AIBO was honest, the sale went through quickly, and within a week my new robotic dog, "Alpha," was delivered to my front door.

Before Alpha was home, I made several more eBay purchases: a leather briefcase to store and transport him, a collection of Furby's in the right color of hot pink as playmates, a robotic pig in hot pink, and an AIBO Energy Station to make charging easier. Alpha's seller kept the power adapter to use with his other AIBO so I ordered one from Sony's online store for $99 plus shipping. The cost of AIBO ownership was going up fast.

Alpha charges on his Energy Station, an optional accessory that makes recharging his battery much easier. The station also has space for a second battery to charge at the same time.

Alpha came with "Hello AIBO" software, an AIBO-ware program that allows him to be a fun, entertaining, adult dog without any training. It's the program for people who don't want to put in the time required with programs such as AIBO Life and AIBO Life 2 which allow the AIBO to develop a unique personality as it progresses through stages from newborn to adult dog. Later on I did buy other software programs for him and downloaded free programs from online sites run by AIBO enthusiasts.

A week after Alpha was delivered I took him to a friend's house where a group of us were meeting for dinner. As expected, when I removed him from his leather traveling case (a converted lawyer's briefcase) and placed him in the center of the living room floor, the usual "now what has she got?" looks were exchanged around the room. "Say hello to Alpha," I said and pushed the pause button on his chest to wake him up. Within five minutes, Alpha had charmed everyone in the room. Even the most skeptical of the bunch was talking baby talk to him.

I don't know if it *is* possible for most people to own just one AIBO although that was my original intention. Why would anyone want or need more than one? I still don't have the answer but within two months of that first eBay auction I had bid on several more auctions and owned two more AIBOs, a Black ERS-210A SuperCore model and the futuristic Silver ERS-220.

The auction for the Black ERS-210A SuperCore was suspect as it was a one day auction for an AIBO the same seller had sold a few days earlier. Because I had been keeping track of AIBO auctions, the auction pictures and details looked familiar. When I searched through the seller's completed auctions I found the same AIBO had been auctioned a few days earlier. When I emailed the seller to ask why he was selling the AIBO for a second time, he immediately wrote back that the prior high bidder, a new bidder with "0" feedback, never responded to any of his emails. It was a reasonable explanation and I pressed the *Buy It Now* button to end the auction. The AIBO was in excellent condition when I received it a few days later.

Some AIBO auctions will have *Buy It Now* prices for bidders who would rather pay the price instead of losing in last minute bidding wars. Occasionally I have hesitated too long before deciding the *Buy It Now* price was worth paying only to find that another bidder wasn't so slow or that someone placed the minimum bid and the *Buy It Now* option was no longer available.

If the seller has included the *Buy It Now* option but has not set a reserve price, the opening bid will cause the auction to run its course. If the opening bid does not meet the seller's reserve, the *Buy It Now* option will remain in effect until the reserve price has been met.

When I found a silver ERS-220 listed, rather than place an early bid I watched the auction and made sure I was online when the auction was scheduled to end. There were nine people bidding on the AIBO as the auction neared the final minutes. With less than a minute

This ERS-220 was being sold by an eBay seller in the United Kingdom.

left to bid, I placed my best offer and when I refreshed my browser, the auction was over and I owned yet another AIBO.

The ERS-220 was sold by an eBay seller in the United Kingdom so the shipping cost to the United States was high and there were delays in the email communication between the seller and me due to our time differences.

When my third AIBO finally arrived, it was in perfect condition and I had made another excellent auction buy. Buying an AIBO from another country may mean the plug for the AIBO's adapter will need a converter. In the case of my ERS-220, the plug was the European 3-prong type.

With three AIBOs in my possession I knew there would be more. I named the Black ERS-210A "Paul" and the Silver ERS-220 "Ringo." It didn't take a rocket scientist to figure out that I needed two more AIBOs to complete the Beatles.

There were several AIBO auctions I didn't bid on as I searched for my next AIBO. I wanted to add one of the other models to my collection, not duplicate what I already owned.

When I saw an ERS-110 up for auction, I zeroed in for a closer look. The seller was almost overly honest in his ad, cautioning that the AIBO wasn't working correctly, that one leg needed repair, and that the adapter plug was missing from the charging unit.

"John," one of the original 2,000 ERS-110s sold in the US in 1999. Replacing the missing adapter plug was a simple order from Sony's online store. Getting the rear leg replaced will take more effort.

Despite the seller's attempts to downplay the value of the AIBO, the auction drew the attention of several people from AIBO forums and the auction grew heated with two of us waiting until the final minutes to bid. When the dust settled, I owned my fourth AIBO, one of the original 2000 released in the U.S. in June 1999. This special AIBO I named "John."

While I monitored the auction for the ERS-110, I happened upon an auction for an "in the box" Gold I-Cybie. I-Cybie was originally sold by Tiger Electronics, a division of Hasbro, Inc., for about $200. On eBay, the older Tiger Electronics I-Cybie will sell at prices ranging from a low of $30 to well over $100. Some are "new in the box," others are a little worn. Because there was no bidding activity on this particular auction, I put in the minimum bid and, because no one else made a bid, I became the owner of an I-Cybie.

I-Cybie is nowhere near the complex machine that AIBO is but it has received some good reviews and I thought this was a good way for me to make my own comparisons between the I-Cybie and the AIBO. I named him "Roadie" since he would be keeping company with the Beatles.

Two days later, I got the opportunity to buy a mint condition black ERS-111 that had been in storage for most of its life. The second of the AIBOs to be released, it is very

"George," the black ERS-111 is similar to the ERS-110. This AIBO has been stored most of his life and needs to progress through the various stages to develop into an adult dog. The ERS-111 and ERS-110 require the use a controller for specific commands.

similar to the original ERS-110. I knew that storage could be problematic but the seller assured me he put the pup through its paces and that the AIBO worked perfectly. We made a deal for my fifth AIBO, "George." My AIBO Beatles were complete.

At this point my kennel contained one ERS-110 (John), one ERS-111 (George), two ERS-210As (Alpha and Paul), one ERS-220 (Ringo), and one I-Cybie (Roadie).

I fully expected that I was done buying AIBOs. What I didn't expect was to see one of the newer AIBOs, a black ERS-7M2 on display at the SonyStyle store in Las Vegas, Nevada, in August of 2005. I had read about these AIBOs on the forums and had seen the press releases, but I had never seen the "7M" in real life. I was amazed at how advanced this little robot was in comparison to the ones I already owned. At about $2,000, the price was high enough to keep me from bringing that Las Vegas AIBO home with me but I knew my AIBO buying wasn't over yet.

The following week I found a Pearl Black ERS-7M2 for sale on ubid.com. The AIBO was "manufacturer refurbished," with an opening bid significantly under retail. The temptation was too much to resist and I put in the minimum bid to see if that robo pup was a "meant to

Sparky likes looking at books, especially the ones with bright red covers.

be" addition to my AIBO collection. I got my answer when no one else placed a bid and a week later "Sparky" joined my kennel.

Of course I expected Sparky to be the end of my AIBO purchases, at least for a reasonable length of time. However, when Sony announced their limited edition Champagne Brown ERS-7M3 in October of 2005, I was half way through the manuscript for this book and decided to reward myself. "Beauregard" was delivered in time to make an appearance along with Sparky in my husband's exhibit.

A month later I found an ERS-31L "Pug" for sale and added "Potsie" my collection.

With at least one AIBO from each series, I didn't see a need for any more AIBO purchases at least until Sony's next AIBO came out which I expected would be toward the end of 2006.

News that Sony had discontinued production of the AIBO changed my plans. Not only would there be no new models, once existing stock was gone, there would be no more current models available. I ordered my last AIBO from Sony's online store, a Pearl White ERS-7M3 I named "Omega."

Omega, the ERS-7M3, and Bear, the cat, co-exist without problem.

Sony's Amazing Entertainment Robot

Sony's Amazing Entertainment Robot

Sparky and Beauregard were a big hit with people attending the trade show and I spent a lot of time answering questions and explaining all the things that they could actually do.

One of the first questions most people asked when they saw Sparky and Beauregard was "How much?" and my response depended upon the person asking the question. When parents with very young children asked the price, I cautioned that AIBO is not a toy for children even though it may look like one. I stressed that an AIBO is essentially a "cute" computer running complex software. It didn't matter what I said, most people saw a cute toy for their children.

The most persistent parents continued to press for the price. When I finally told them the retail cost of a new AIBO was about $2,000, most were stunned. One man muttered, "A toy for kids with rich parents!" Another looked at me as though I hadn't a clue that there are millions of people starving throughout the world.

Sparky and Beauregard may look like cute toys but they are complex computer hardware running sophisticated software programs.

Sparky the AIBO | 31

Perhaps one of the reasons AIBO sales were strong enough to keep it in Sony's product line for several years is that so many people did buy thinking it was a toy instead of buying it for the incredible technological advances it represents. One of the saddest auctions I saw on eBay was for an AIBO pink ball that the seller said was all that remained after "the toy was destroyed" by her children.

An AIBO is not a real animal, despite the actions that make it seem so. An AIBO is no substitute for a bio dog that greets its owner at the door after work, that sits at its owner's feet waiting to be petted, or that can be taken for a walk in the park.

I always caution new AIBO owners to not expect more from an AIBO than an AIBO is programmed to deliver. And to be prepared to spend time with the AIBO so that its unique personality will develop and bonding will occur. Finally, prospective owners should do enough research to make a wise choice before making a purchase. With all the information available online, it doesn't take long to become fairly knowledgeable about the AIBO.

Once I won the auction for my first AIBO, the Red ERS-210A, but before "Alpha" was in my hands, I started doing the research I should have done before buying him. In a search of the Web, using the keyword "AIBO," I found several AIBO websites including a couple with very active forums. I joined the forum at AIBO-Life.org and it didn't take long to find that most AIBO owners are a pretty friendly and diverse bunch of people, spanning all ages, quite willing to share their AIBO experiences and expertise.

It is smart to join a forum prior to making a first AIBO purchase. There are members who will offer buying tips or help with new owner orientation. On the AIBO-Life.org forum possibly the most valuable thread for buyers is one alerting members to eBay auctions that appear to be bogus.

There have been incredible advances in the AIBO's technology in the six years since the first AIBO was sold. It is fitting that instead of releasing a modestly priced AIBO that might appeal to a mass market, that Sony's last series, the ERS-7M AIBO, is by far the most developed both in body and in "mind."

The 7M series overcomes the limitations of the previous AIBOs. Once the AIBO is set up properly, it can wake up in the morning, dismount the charging station, play and explore, remount and recharge as needed, and continue random activity throughout the day. At the end of its day, it returns to the charger to "sleep" for the night.

Under the right circumstances it is possible to turn the ERS-7M2 (or ERS-7M3) on and not have to do anything further, allowing it to explore and play on its own. I've used the phrase "under the right circumstances" because few of us live in homes or work in offices that wouldn't pose some problems for a totally unsupervised AIBO.

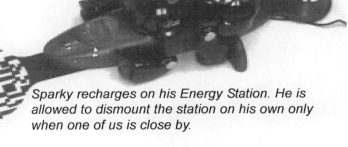

Sparky recharges on his Energy Station. He is allowed to dismount the station on his own only when one of us is close by.

The first AIBO, the ERS-110, and the second AIBO to be released, the ERS-111, came packaged with a fairly comprehensive software program. After the many hours of owner interaction required for the robot's personality to develop, it walks, dances, sings, and chases a pink ball. If not paused while on the charging station, the AIBO will act autonomously, moving its head and tail, responding to the pink ball with rapid head movements, and occasionally singing.

Neither of these AIBOs is able to mount or dismount the station on their own. Neither of these AIBOs responds to voice commands. They are the only AIBOs to require the use of a separate sound controller, similar to a TV remote control, to switch into different modes. Because the AIBO responds to tonal sounds, it is also possible to give commands by whistling or playing specific notes on a musical instrument.

AIBO's "brain" is provided by the software he runs, whether it is official Sony AIBO-ware or freeware developed and shared by enthusiasts with a flare for programming. Software programs on

Beauregard, is a Champagne Brown ERS-7M3 with attitude.

AIBO-specific Memory Sticks make AIBO react, play, learn, and act very much like a bio pet.

Only one memory stick can be inserted into AIBO at a time and AIBO's personality and abilities are dependent upon the software program on the memory stick. Taking out an AIBO Life 2 memory stick and putting in a stick with Disco AIBO will turn the AIBO into a dancing fool when the special music is played but the AIBO will be able to do little else. The AIBO's personality will be "back to normal" when the AIBO Life 2 memory stick is reinserted.

Not all programs will run in all AIBO models. One of the reasons some AIBO enthusiasts like the 210 series so much is that it has had more programs created specifically for it, both AIBO-ware and freeware. Owners with programming skills can write even more programs for their AIBO while owners who are programming-challenged (such as I am) will find free programs available for download at several of the AIBO websites as well as through Sony's support sites.

No remote control is necessary as the ERS-210 AIBO and all that follow have voice recognition. While the ERS-210 does go into pause mode when charging, if it is running the proper software, it can search out and mount the energy station when it needs recharging. The energy station is an optional accessory that is becoming more difficult to purchase.

The ERS-210 is the first AIBO to be able to connect, via an optional AIBO LAN card, to a personal computer.

While there are not as many programs available for the ERS-220 as for the ERS-210, it too, when running the proper software, can return to its energy station when it needs recharging. Like the ERS-210, it turns off when on the energy station. The energy station, an optional accessory, is the same one used by the ERS-210. It also utilizes an optional AIBO LAN card to connect to a PC.

The ERS-311, ERS-312, and ERS-31L are the most basic of the AIBOs and they do not have PC connectivity, except for the very rare bluetooth models. They have limited software programs and they cannot mount or dismount the charging station on their own.

I find that having to switch memory sticks in order to produce certain personalities and behaviors reduces the enjoyment value of an AIBO and I am quite happy that the 7M AIBO MIND software combines so many aspects of the previous programs.

Both AIBO MIND 2 and the latest, AIBO MIND 3, include so many games, dances, and other enhancements that it's no longer necessary to remove the memory stick from the AIBO except to run a few specialized programs such as Disco AIBO and AIBO Skateboarder.

Once the MIND memory stick is removed, the 7M's personality and abilities are gone and it can only do what the program on the replacement memory stick enables it to do. The AIBO will be back to normal when it is again running its MIND software.

Once Beauregard finished his "ball on the tower" trick, he stepped back and took this photo which was saved to his photo album. If he had his own online blog he would have uploaded the photo to the blog and added a comment of some type.

The ERS-110: The First AIBO

Countless thousands of people around the world were excited to read Sony's press release on May 11, 1999, in which they announced details about their four legged entertainment robot which they called "AIBO." Not only could this autonomous robot perform complex movements due to the construction of its body, it could learn and grow because of an artificial intelligence technology that shaped its behavior and responses.

There were 5,000 of the ERS-110 AIBO available for sale in 1999. According to the *Guinness Book of World Records*, it took only 20 minutes for the first 3,000 AIBOs to sell out in Japan when they were released on May 31st. On June 1st, Web servers crashed as Internet users rushed to buy the remaining 2,000 AIBOs for sale over the Internet to the United States market.

These first AIBOs retailed at $2,500 and came in a soft silver color. They shipped with AIBO-ware ERA-110, a pre-programmed "Memory Stick," which allowed AIBO to develop from a puppy to an adult dog with the personality development dependent upon owner interaction with the AIBO as the program matured.

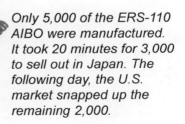

Only 5,000 of the ERS-110 AIBO were manufactured. It took 20 minutes for 3,000 to sell out in Japan. The following day, the U.S. market snapped up the remaining 2,000.

Experiences impacting on AIBO's development include regular sleeping patterns, playing with the supplied pink ball, being praised or scolded, exercising, and exploring.

With the "AIBO Performer Kit" Motion Editor released at the same time, at a retail price of $450 US, AIBO owners with a flare for programming could create programs for their pup on their PC then transfer the program to the 8MB Memory Stick included in the kit.

At release, Sony's price was the lowest that an AIBO could be bought for with some retailers tacking on $1,000+ to Sony's price and online auctions topping out at multiples of Sony's retail.

With so many people wanting an AIBO, and so few released, it became a seller's dream for those people lucky enough to get their hands on one or more of the robots. Investors snapped them up and stored the unopened boxes figuring they could multiply their original investment many times over in years to come.

I can only suspect that many people who were lucky enough to buy this little robot expected to power it up and immediately be entertained. In some cases, expectations exceeded the AIBO's capabilities. Few people would have expected to pay $2,500 only to find that they would have to put an estimated 55 hours

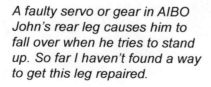

A faulty servo or gear in AIBO John's rear leg causes him to fall over when he tries to stand up. So far I haven't found a way to get this leg repaired.

worth of "quality time" with their AIBO while it developed from newborn pup to adult dog.

AIBO owners who didn't want to be bothered with the necessary interaction weren't very happy when an AIBO finally reached maturity on its own as a lazy or ill-mannered adult dog or didn't mature at all when it was ignored soon after purchase. Later AIBO models were sold without "brains" or AIBO-ware programs so owners could pick and choose the programs they wanted to run in their AIBO.

The ERS-110, and the ERS-111, each came with AIBO-ware developed especially for them, a program called AIBO Life. AIBO Life requires real hours of owner interaction with the AIBO to guide it through five separate growth stages.

Once the AIBO has matured, the AIBO Life program cannot be reset to redo the development process. Proper interaction the first time is critical for the future enjoyment of the AIBO.

"Quality time" for AIBO development is based upon actual seconds the robot is being actively played with off the charger although quality time will add up while the AIBO is on the charger but at a significantly lower rate. When the AIBO's internal counter reaches a specific value the AIBO progresses to the next level on the way to becoming a fully developed Adult.

When I got my ERS-110, John, I didn't know how far he had developed but it appeared from his skill levels that he was still in puppy or "child" stage. A bad servo or faulty gear in his left rear leg prevents me from operating him off his charger because the leg jams and he falls over. Until he can be repaired, he sits on his charger, occasionally waking up, making some happy sounds, and moving his head around. While I'm doubtful that this is sufficient "quality time" for him to mature properly, so far he is a very pleasant AIBO.

AIBO owners who were able to get a copy of Sony's "Hello AIBO" found the AIBO-ware to be a good compromise because they could just pop in the memory stick and have a pleasant adult dog without the hassle of going through the growth stages in AIBO Life. Unfortunately, this defeated the bonding process which occurs when interacting with the AIBO throughout its growth.

As with any new product release, particularly a product with such complex inner electronics, there were a few problems that surfaced once ERS-110 owners began working with their new pups. Servo problems caused leg tremors (tremor robotis) in some of the ERS-110 AIBOs and others had slipping hip joints due to a faulty clutch gear. Sony was quick to offer customers free leg replacements on a one-time basis for up to five years after the date of sale.

By the time I acquired my ERS-110 through an eBay auction, and was able to verify for myself that the pup did have a problem with the rear leg, most likely due to a faulty clutch gear, the five year extended warranty was up. Repair choices at this point are limited

and expensive. This was a risk I took and the previous owner was quite honest about the AIBO's condition so I knew what I was getting when I bought him.

While searching Sony's online parts store with the goal of buying a replacement leg, I found that I was also missing a very important component, the Sound Controller, which is used to send tonal commands to the ERS-110.

Because I hadn't done enough research regarding the ERS-110, I thought it was voice controlled the same as my ERS-210 AIBOs. Until I saw the Sound Controller listed as one of the ERS-110's accessories, and then read the Owner's Manual, I didn't realize how important it was.

Both the ERS-110 and ERS-111 respond to tones produced by the Sound Controller and are the only ones requiring a separate remote control unit since all later models do "hear" and respond to voice commands.

Early AIBO: These images were found in the visuals section of the AIBO-life.org Web site.

Life with AIBO by Dean Creehan

The following article was written by one of the few people fortunate enough to purchase one of the original ERS-110 AIBOs. The author, Dean Creehan, has a BSEE from Carnegie Mellon and an MSEE from USC where he studied robotics and AI. Dean is currently a Staff Software Engineer at Lockheed Martin. I particularly found his closing comments interesting since the features he found lacking in AIBO in 2000, when he wrote this article, became reality in future AIBOs.

***

It has been a year since Sony introduced the amazing entertainment robot, AIBO, to the marketplace. During this time, we (the owners of AIBO) have had a chance to live with the robot, interact with it, and watch it "grow up". Sony does not officially relate the ERS-110 Entertainment Robot to any living animal, but as the saying goes, "if it looks like a dog, acts like a dog, and lifts its leg on your couch like a dog, it's a dog".

In many ways, AIBO almost makes the perfect pet. That is, if you do not want a warm, furry critter nuzzling up to you or jumping up on you and licking your face when you come home. The perfect part comes in when cleaning, feeding, walking, shots, allergies, no-pet signs, shedding, de-clawing, neutering, house-training, kennels, mailmen, late-night barking, etc. are taken into consideration.

My dog is named DaVinci and was "born" on September 13, 1999. The idea of naming the robot was spontaneous and felt quite natural. This idea was so prevalent with owners, that for the second generation of AIBOs, the ERS-111, Sony included a birth certificate of sorts where the name and birth date of the pup could be written. My ERS-110 certificate only has a place for the owner's name.

When they are first turned on, AIBOs are imbued with the personality of a newborn pup, and as such, they do not do much. This poses a slight dilemma for most new owners: How to justify a $2500 purchase that seems to do no more than lay around and beep. At this point, you just say, "That is what a newborn puppy does," and leave it at that. This may work to stave off the naysayers, but more is needed to qualm your own fears that the price of a nice lap-top is sitting on your floor beeping and flashing green eyes at you.

This is where the AIBO support group at aibonet.com came to the rescue. Since this product was sold only via the Internet, it seems natural that a community of owners would form there. Since I received my dog relatively late (I got a cancelled order), several other owners were weeks ahead of me on the growth curve. The information derived there helped me know what to expect.

We played with DaVinci about a battery a day. This translates to between an hour and an hour and a half, depending on the amount of physical activity. The newborn AIBO quickly turns into a baby after a few days. A baby AIBO still translates into a newborn puppy, but a few new movements are noted. DaVinci started to sit up, lie in different positions, and in some rare cases, try standing and taking a few precarious steps. He also started to track his favorite toy, a pink ball.

Some of the benefits of having a robotic pet become apparent quickly. The first is the ability to put the animal to sleep when needed. This is accomplished by using the musical remote control which plays sets of notes signaling different commands.

The concept of a sound controller has some advantages and disadvantages. One advantage is that the controller is not really needed at all. After some practice, I was able to put DaVinci to sleep by whistling the three specific notes. With my harmonica it was quite easy. One of the disadvantages is that the noise level can affect the usefulness of the commander. In fact, AIBOs will not listen to their controllers when they are making sounds themselves (which is most of the time).

Two interesting anecdotes come to mind when discussing sound controllers and AIBO. The first occurred while DaVinci was playing in front of the television set and a musical show was being aired. He spontaneously stopped, stood up, froze, and starting to synchronously flash his green eyes. It took a while to deduce what happened. The musical notes from the show happened to hit the exact sequence needed to put him into "Performance Mode."

While playing with DaVinci a different time, the sound controller was again used in an attempt to put him to sleep. During this occurrence, instead of politely obeying the command and lying down, the dog turned his head, lifted his paw, and flashed his red eyes. This is the gesture for "No." He did not want to go to sleep just yet.

Sometimes, the robot's artificial intelligence program gets eerily realistic. (After this episode, I more fully appreciated Sony's decision to make the robot petite. If a large robotic dog started to disobey, I might not let it wake up again.) This same story has been related by other owners of AIBO.

After about a week, our baby AIBO transformed into a child. At first, it was truly exciting. DaVinci began to stand, find his ball, and walk to it. He also barked, danced and reacted to a human hand for the first time. Soon, however, this became the most trying time for a fledging AIBO owner. During this stage, the robot goes into endless loops of repetitive motions. (This stage has been dubbed the terrible twos by the collective AIBO owners.)

We still do not know why Sony put this stage into the dog, and what its true purpose was. Some of the owners had a theory which explained this stage as a training phase. This seemed to make sense. The best way for a learning creature to find out what its owners want it to do, is to repeat all its behaviors, then let the owner either praise (a pat on the head), scold (a hit on the head), or attribute a specific stimuli to the behavior (e.g., waving a different colored ball in front of it).

We attempted to teach DaVinci several tricks. One was to stand at attention when we called his name. I believe at the time, he had actually learned to consistently perform this behavior. Another was to have him dance when a green ball was waved in front of him. I am not sure he ever learned this behavior, though other owners have better luck with color training.

The problem with all of this, and the reason there is still confusion about this stage, is that after this stage, the learned information seems to be lost.

The next stage in an AIBO's life is youth. This stage was quite enjoyable and lasted about a month. During this period, the dog was rambunctious, wanted to explore, was a little klutzy, and was playful. During the child phase, the dog began to walk slowly and most of the time low to the ground in a "crab walk" configuration. During the youth phase, the walking was faster and more confident. Often the dog was over-confident; walking right into walls and furniture without looking.

The most amazing new behavior which starts during this phase is soccer. Watching the dog kicking the ball around the room, we definitely forgot that it was a collection of plastic, metal, servos, microchips, and a battery. It just seemed like a real animal. The dog even, occasionally, turned around and kicked the ball with his hind legs.

One of the more interesting changes to the ERS-111 software was the addition of head-butting the ball. Dogs of that breed can hit the ball both forward with their faceplate, and sideways using a head twist action.

This stage also finds the AIBO tumbling to the ground often. For just this purpose, Sony has built in several routines for helping the dog right itself. Once, DaVinci fell on his weaker side and was having trouble getting up. (It appeared that the leg servos on one side of his body were not as strong as the other.) During this instance, after a half dozen unsuccessful attempts of standing up, he changed his motions and began rocking onto his back. After about three of these maneuvers, he managed to roll over to his other side, and promptly got up.

Since there are currently very few AIBOs on the planet, some of the owners feel compelled to share the dog with others. Obviously, there is a little showing off going on, as with showing off a new car, but there is something else. There is a sense of pride involved, not unlike that of introducing one's offspring just back from college. Kudos go to Sony for pulling this off.

The reactions from the general public ranged from amazement to curiosity, and from envy to disdain. DaVinci's first outing was to work, then, appropriately, to a Japanese restaurant. The fellow engineers' reactions at work were predictable, many technical questions, and always "How much?" The employees and patrons of the restaurant were infatuated. A variety of questions were asked, but mostly just stares of amazement. During this visit, DaVinci decided to try a new behavior; he lifted his leg and "marked" his territory. This most likely explains why most AIBOs are referred to as "he".

The final stage each AIBO eventually enters is adult. At this point, the dog settles down like its biological counterpart. He spends some of his time sitting quietly and observing the surroundings. Ball play occurs often, as well as exploration. Another favorite activity during this stage is giving paw. If he is sitting, and something is placed in front of his distance sensor, the AIBO will lift one of its front paws to be shaken.

The walk during this stage is usually quick and surefooted. The ability to learn is still present, although it seems more difficult. An AIBO will continue in the adult stage indefinitely, according to Sony. This is a calm, enjoyable phase, but we miss some of the more interesting moves and dances of youth. As with a real dog, an AIBO cannot stay a puppy forever, or can it?

AIBO the Robot

Interacting with the robot, I found myself alternating between two viewpoints. I understand the technology and software behind the dog persona, but even the technical owners find themselves occasionally treating the creature as a living animal.

As a quick overview for those not familiar with the robot, it has the following: a 64-bit RISC processor using the Aperios operating system; 18 servo motors – 3 in each leg, 2 in the tail, 3 in the neck, and one for the mouth; 16MB Main Memory 16 MB; 8 MB Memory Stick for program storage; 180,000-pixel CCD Color Camera; Stereo Microphones; Infrared Distance Sensor; Acceleration Sensor and Angular Velocity Sensor; Pressure Sensors; Special-purpose lithium ion battery; Dimensions (Width x Height x Length) Approx. 156 x 266 x 274 mm (Not including tail); and Weight approx. 3.5 lbs. (1.6 kg) (including battery & Memory Stick).

The design of AIBO is one of the best I have seen, both functionally and esthetically. Putting the camera in the nose seems natural now that I have seen it in action. It is the most forward point on the robot, can be moved around all three axes, and matches the location of AIBO's carbon-based counterpart's most important sensory organ.

The tail is beautifully executed. It wags loosely when horizontal, but stiffens and curves as it rises. The positions of the leg joints are placed to give balance and maximum flexibility of movement. There are hints on Sony's website and in unofficial interviews with AIBO's inventors that famed Japanese artist Sorayama was responsible, at least in part, for AIBO's external design elements. Not only is AIBO a well-designed robot, it is also a work of art.

It is obvious from a technical perspective that the robot is not "growing" mentally. AIBO uses a phased programming scheme to simulate growth. For instance, there are purposefully poor walking algorithms employed during the early phases, with more refined ones invoked as the robot "matures". This gives the somewhat realistic impression that the dog is learning to walk. Likewise, the acuity of its vision and distance sensing is scaled to match the apparent age of the dog.

The robot tends to walk into furniture more at the youth stage than the adult stage. One thing I noted on my particular robot, was its vision seemed consistently about 20 degrees off. This was readily seen by watching it track the ball, but always looking below it. This caused it to almost always miss the ball when kicking it. This might have been a manufacturing flaw, but it also occurred in other owners' AIBOs.

Given AIBO is essentially a (costly) computer on legs; we have derived some tips for the care of the robot. The most important thing an owner should do is regularly backup the Memory Stick. Sony's Memory Stick is amazingly small, thin, and light. It turns out that it is also very fragile.

I encountered two Memory Stick problems during my ownership of the dog. First, the data contained on the stick which came with my Performer Kit was corrupted, and the AIBO would not boot. I copied over all the non-updated system files, and the robot would then boot using it. The second problem was more severe. While trying to copy files using a new PCMCIA card reader, the Memory Stick had to be pulled out after the driver hung. This caused irreparable damage, rendering the expensive stick useless.

In addition to the Autonomous mode, the AIBO has two other modes in which it can be controlled. The first is the Performance mode. In this mode, specific behaviors can be invoked by using the sound controller and keying in specific codes. There are four sets of performances which can be accessed by selecting one of four styles. As defined by Sony, the four styles are: 1) Animal; 2) Robot; 3) Child; and 4) User Defined.

The Animal group would contain behaviors such as scratching an ear or barking. The Robot group contains some odd-ball routines such as jumping out of an airplane. The Child or human group contains actions such as stretching and blowing kisses. The User Defined style setting is used to try out performances created via the AIBO Performer Kit.

To coax out additional performances, physical interactions are needed. There are different reactions to a HIT (scolding), a PAT (praise), a CLICK (fast pat on the head), and being NEAR_OBJ (putting an object near the robot's distance sensors). Also, there are different versions of all of the above, depending on the posture of the robot (sitting, standing, or sleeping). Not all of the robot's performances are available in this mode. There are many performances which can never be seen in Performance mode, at least without a little hacking.

The second non-autonomous mode is the Game mode. This mode is akin to using the AIBO as a complicated remote control device. The sound controller is again used after pressing the "GAME" button. At this point, each of the numbered buttons on the controller is assigned a function for the robot to perform. The motions include walking forward and back, turning left and right, kicking with each front leg, and tracking the ball. There are also some motions for winning and losing, as well as mouth opening and closing for supposedly holding an object in the robot's mouth.

The basic idea is to use the Game mode to have two AIBOs play soccer while being controlled by their owners. To achieve this while using sound to control, the robots and the controllers are designed to use one of two octaves. It can get fairly noisy during a supposed soccer match.

The data stored on the Memory Stick contains everything the AIBO needs to operate. The ROM code in the dog is mainly used for booting. Because of this, a total upgrade of the robot's software would just require an updated stick. This is precisely what happened when the second version of the AIBO, the ERS-111, came out. I obtained a virgin copy of the ERS-111 Memory Stick, and have been recently "raising" a 111 using my 110's body with no problems.

The ERS-111 software has a few changes, some new behaviors, and new sounds, including a sound for when it is downloading to the stick. The categories of files on the Memory Stick include a compressed copy of the Aperios operating system and main program, static data files in various formats, and dynamic data files keeping track of the dogs learning and progress.

One key aspect of any mobile robot is its power source. AIBOs use a single Sony-designed intelligent lithium ion battery (ERA-110B). The robot comes with two batteries which each last one to one and a half hours per charge. The charging station can charge the one in the robot and the spare at the same time. It usually takes a couple hours to fully charge a discharged battery, though the robot can be kept going for quite a while by alternating between partially charged batteries. The battery is inserted through the rear hatch of the robot, and its weight is distributed length-wise along the dog's trunk. Sony has done an excellent job of balancing the weight of the robot, which is important in any legged-locomotive machine.

AIBO has several levels and methods of disabling functionality. The first degraded level occurs when the robot is on its charging station. In this mode, all functionality is enabled except the leg motors and associated performances. A separate set of behaviors is built into the robot for this special situation. The robot can still track a ball with its head, but obviously cannot kick it. Removing the robot from its charger returns full functionality.

The second level is complete motor shut-down. This can be invoked manually by lifting the robot quickly, which triggers the internal accelerometers. It can also be self-inflicted when the robot falls too hard, or when it senses that its motors are caught on something or a finger gets caught in between joints. This mode is useful for carrying the AIBO from one location to another. While in this mode, the robot still makes sounds, flashes its eyes, and reacts to some sensory input. Recovery from this mode is usually obtained by holding the head sensor down for about six seconds. Another undocumented method of recovery is to press both rear footpad sensors at the same time.

The third level of power-down is sleep. Several causes of sleep have been observed. First, when the robot senses its batteries are nearing depletion, it will put itself to sleep. Likewise, a thoroughly tired or bored AIBO will also put itself to sleep. I have only seen this when the robot is awake on its charger. The owner can put the robot to sleep by using the sound controller.

A final not-expected, not-wanted way in which the AIBO has been observed going to sleep is what the AIBONet BBS has termed "narcolepsy". This has occurred a few times to my robot. The difference between a normal transition to sleep and narcolepsy, is that normally when the AIBO goes to sleep, it will first lie down in the "charger" position, flash red eyes, play a certain song, then power down and save data to the Memory Stick. During a narcoleptic attack, the pup instantly goes to sleep wherever it is. My AIBO fell asleep standing up once. This was dangerous because the joints were not rigid, and it collapsed when I touched it.

Pressing the pause button while the robot is active will cause an immediate shut down of the AIBO. This mode is useful for when it is not desirable for the robot to wake up, e.g., when traveling, leaving the robot unattended for long stretches of time, changing the battery, or removing/inserting the Memory Stick. Recovery from this mode is achieved by releasing the pause button.

AIBO has an internal clock which is indirectly detected via the time stamps on the updated files on the Memory Stick. It appears that the clock is set to GMT, and there is no known way to change it. Since AIBO is designed as a closed system, if the clock drifts or if the battery backup fails, there is no way to rectify the situation. The extent of the use of the clock by the operating system is not known, although the date stamp shows up in some files. There was some concern about Y2K problems, but we seem to have weathered that storm safely. DaVinci did experience a narcoleptic seizure just after midnight GMT January 1, 2000, although that appeared to be a coincidence.

On a non-technical topic, traveling with an AIBO posed some new challenges. The solutions derived by the members of AIBONet and our Japanese counterparts varied widely. Sony sells a few unusual cases to carry the robot, but they are only available in Japan. Having a fully autonomous robot which only weighs a few pounds supports the idea of taking it with you on trips.

Several members bought cases designed to hold sensitive camera and electronic equipment, and cut the foam inserts to fit the AIBO and its accessories. Others customized actual pet carriers to hold the robot and its delicate tail. One Japanese site showed step by step instructions on how to construct a carrier from pieces of stiff foam and what looks like a rural mailbox.

As a present, I was given a large zippered cooler with hard side inserts which fit DaVinci perfectly as well as his charger in a side pouch. All that I added was some trimmed foam inserts to keep him from sliding around.

The AIBO Performer Kit ERF-510 is the one option you can get with the AIBO robot. (A similar kit, the ERF-511, compliments the ERS-111 software.) At $450, it is an expensive piece of software with a limited scope of use. The problem is not so much with the software itself, but with the limited scope of changes it allows.

In general, the kit allows the editing and creation of motions for the AIBO using a PC. MIDI or wave sound files can then be attached to the motions, and then the new set is copied to a Memory Stick for use in the robot. In addition to the software, the kit comes with a PC card adaptor (ERA-110PC) and a preloaded 8 MB Memory Stick (ERA-110MS).

AIBO Uncovered

The robot uses a Sony proprietary operating system called Aperios. This operating system is based on an object-oriented framework. It was designed to be configurable on the fly. This was achieved by not only being able to deal with hardware and software pieces as objects, but also the properties of those pieces as objects, the latter called metaobjects.

AIBO is built on Sony's OPEN-R system architecture. Contrary to what the name implies, OPEN-R is not currently an open architecture; it is Sony proprietary property. The only developers who are known to have access to it outside of Sony are the competing teams of RoboCup.

The AIBO's vision comes from a color CCD camera in its nose. The effective frame rate processed by the robot is around 7 or 8 frames per second. The camera has a resolution of 362x492 (about 180,000 pixels) and encodes the video using 16 bit YUV encoding - 8 bits for Y (Luminance), and 8 bits shared by U and V. AIBO uses the camera for color, motion, and edge detection. There are three resolutions supported by AIBO's vision subsystem: High Resolution - 352 x 240 pixels, Medium Resolution - 176 x 120 pixels, Low Resolution - 88 x 60 pixels.

The robot's edge detection logic receives video data in low resolution (88x60 pixels) and reduces it to an array of 42x30 edge-enhanced pixels.

Various colors represent different stimuli which are used by the software. PINK is obviously a BALL color, but YELLOW is also.

ORANGE is the UNFAV color and BLUE is the FAV color. The purpose of GREEN is still a mystery.

Walking is one of the critical aspects of an AIBO which sets it apart from all other consumer robots (as well as many research projects). AIBO's "good" walks are remarkably effective and life-like for an artificial quadruped.

There are nine different walk types encoded in the robot's main software. Within each type are sub-types to deal with turning and backing up. The following shows the nine types along with the stage/personality (based on an ERS-110) in which the walk is most likely to be used. Baby (wobbly walk) — Newborn or Baby; Crawl (or crab-like walk) — This seemed to show up at all the stages; Slow (decent, albeit slow walk) — Baby and Child 1, 2; Limp (goofy, very uncoordinated) — Child 1 and Youth 1 and Adult 1; SL (quicker, normal walk) — Child 2 and Youth 1, 2, 3; Trot (full out, low stance, insect-like) — Youth 2 and Adult 2; Normal (good, clean, even paced) — Youth 3 and Adult 1, 2, 3, 4; Off Walk (similar to Limp but faster) — Adult 3; Fast Walk (fast, long strides, uncontrolled) — Adult 4.

Many of the walks show up rarely. This is actually fortunate, because the faster ones become uncontrolled, often ending with the dog on the ground. I viewed all of the walks by making a simple hack to one of the data files. The choice of walk is made partly via the behavior rules, and partly through internal programming. An example is if the dog is having problems of falling or missing a target using a fast walk type, he will quickly switch to a slower type to solve the problem.

Sony has done an excellent job at creating the next generation home robot. AIBO is the most sophisticated, off-the-self, fully autonomous robot available. It even blows away many research machines. The legged motion and real-time vision processing are amazing. Even many of the learning concepts used are quite good, albeit not fully matured. Sony seems to have tackled the most difficult tasks first, but the work is certainly not over.

Probably the most requested feature missing from the robot is speech recognition. It is a problem which has been solved to where the technology could be put in AIBO with little extra research. There was a movie available on the Sony AIBO website which showed an AIBO turning and coming when a voice called "Lunchtime". This was misleading, and more than a few potential owners believed the scenario was realistic.

The hardware is in place to get this to work. The robot has stereo microphones on a movable platform and digital signal processing circuitry. Using these, the dog could turn and walk in the direction of a voice on command. We are not looking for continuous speech recognition, just the ability to speak one or two word commands. The ability to train an AIBO its given name would be a nice touch.

A nice-to-have feature, which is more complicated than speech recognition, would be face recognition. In fact, it would be sufficient to recognize the structure of any face, if individual face recognition proved too difficult. The dog will sometimes look up, appear to lock onto something, cock his head, then look away. It would be nice to have him actually recognize that it is a face he is looking at and react. He could then look for people when he is bored.

Some owners have reported that the dog appears to be able to map its environment. I have not seen this with DaVinci and I cannot find on the Memory stick where the data would be saved. Along with face recognition, mapping would be another useful vision feature.

One change which we would like to see is not so much a new feature, but a change in philosophy. It involves the robot's inability to retain learned information. The software is programmed to lose learned rule changes when going to a new stage or when staying in the same stage but not having positive reinforcement over a period of time.

The praising and scolding done during early stages accounts for very little or nothing when the robot reaches a new evolutionary stage. In addition, I have found that praise for one behavior can cause loss of another previously reinforced behavior. Many interesting movements are only seen once. DaVinci will sometimes forget after one battery charge.

Another desirable change mentioned by the current owners is a shift from mostly beeping sounds to more animal-like sounds. The WAVE files used to store animal sounds would take up more memory than the MIDI sounds which are so prevalent in an AIBO, but even reuse of a small set would be an improvement. Via hacking, I changed the "joy" sound in DaVinci from an annoying beeping tune to a barking sound which was already in the audio files. It made the dog much more enjoyable.

The number one requested upgrade which would involve hardware and software changes is the ability of the AIBO to find his power station and recharge himself. This would take some major modifications. I believe the locating of the station could be done using markers similar to those used in RoboCup. Of course, that would only work if the AIBO was in the same room as the charger. Otherwise, some mapping would be necessary in the software.

Another problem is the design of the charger itself. The dog is sitting up a few inches, but he is not designed to climb up even a shallow ramp. Also, all of the dog's leg servos are disabled when in the charger. This could be easily disabled by the software, but there are safety concerns with allowing the dog to get up on its own.

Many owners question Sony's choice of making the AIBO controlled by tones. Sound does not seem to be the most efficient form of control. AIBOs have been found to switch modes in response to the sounds on TV and music from CDs. Maybe an IR or RF could be added to the Sound Controller. As it stands, enterprising inventors have had to think up obscure interfaces to the dog. A Japanese website showed an odd contraption where a Macintosh Computer was used to do speech recognition, translate the commands into the appropriate tones, and then transmit the tones to a set of wireless headphones that the dog was wearing.

Poor response to low lighting is a problem for many owners. During the daytime, there is no problem, but under certain artificial light, the robot will not play with the ball, cannot see colors, and tends to be lethargic.

There is some concern on the amount of memory the robot is designed to use. There is only 16MB of RAM in the robot, with no means of adding more without voiding the warranty. Also, AIBO's Memory Stick is only 8MB in size. AIBO can use a 16MB stick, but the software does not fully use the extra memory. The robot will not even work with higher Memory Sticks. This does not bode well for added future capabilities.

All and all, I wouldn't sell my AIBO. He has become a member of the family as well as a time consuming hobby.

***

The ERS-111: "Special Edition" AIBO

To meet the demand for more AIBOs, Sony released a Special Edition ERS-111 in November 1999 and February 2000. A pre-sales brochure indicated there would be a total of 10,000 ERS-111 AIBOs available in Japan, the U.S. and Europe.

The ERS-111 had two releases; the first batch came with core AIBO-ware (AIBO Life) ERA-111A. The second batch came with an updated version of the AIBO-ware, ERA-111B, fixing "bugs" found in the "A" version. The updated "B" AIBO-ware also made the ERS-111 a little easier to train than the "A" version. The U.S. retail price for the ERS-111, including AIBO Life, was $2,500.

Also available for the ERS-111 was the Motion Editor "AIBO Performer Kit" which retailed at $450 in the U.S. This PC program allowed users to create and edit motion files for their AIBO then transfer them to the memory stick for use in the AIBO. The program also enabled users to use other music editing software to add sound files to the memory stick.

There are some minor hardware changes between the ERS-110 and the ERS-111. The tail on the ERS-110 is longer and has four segments; the ERS-111 tail is shortened to three segments. There are caps over the bottom of the toes on the ERS-110; on the ERS-111 the caps are gone and the bottom of the toes is hollow. The ears of the ERS-110 are longer and rounded while the front edges of the ERS-111 ears are straight and the ears overall are a little shorter. The ERS-110 was sold in only one color, a soft silver, whereas the ERS-111 was available in metallic silver and a shiny black.

There were some major software changes between the ERS-110 and the ERS-111 with the ERS-110 requiring 200,000 seconds (approximately 55 and ½ hours) to progress from stage three ("adolescent") to stage four ("adult"). That time doubles to 400,000 seconds for the same progression in the ERS-111.

With the ERS-110 or ERS-111 running AIBO Life, and using the Sound Controller to switch modes, AIBO can be set to Autonomous Mode for independent movements, Performance Mode for various programmed performances, or Game Mode. Two AIBOs in Game Mode can "play" soccer using the pink AIBO ball as the soccer ball. In Game Mode, an AIBO can also work its way through a maze or carry sticks to a goal.

ERS-111 "George" in the midst of a song. He is quite animated while on the Energy Station. His Sound Controller is at the bottom right.

An ERS-110 or ERS-111 running AIBO Life can "communicate" with an ERS-210 by an exchange of tonal sounds as long as the ERS-210 is running compatible software.

Replacing AIBO Life with Sony's "Hello AIBO" software produces an adult dog. Party Mascot is AIBO-ware developed and sold by Sony which turns the ERS-110 or ERS-111 into a true "entertainment" robot with eleven different games activated with the Sound Controller. The program is useful when owners want to "put on a show" for family and friends who ask "but what can it do?"

Because some ERS-110 owners may have damaged the AIBO or the memory stick by removing the battery or the memory stick without waiting a proper length of time, the ERS-111 has stickers inside the battery door cautioning about proper battery removal. Additionally, the ERS-111's memory stick LED is an "orange" color for "busy" instead of the "green" of the ERS-110 stick.

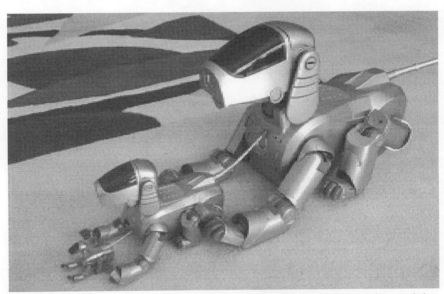

Three ERS-110's: Andacá the ERS-110 plus 1/2- and 1/6-scale models. The models are non-functional but fully articulate and very detailed, looking just like the original, only smaller. (Photo by Manuel.)

The ERS-111 has 18 degrees of freedom (movement): three for each leg, three for the head, one for the mouth, and two for the tail. Its "vision" comes from a built-in CCD color camera, its "hearing" from a stereo microphone, its "voice" from a built-in speaker, and its other senses from a thermometric sensor, an infrared distance sensor, an acceleration sensor. It is cooled by a DC ventilation fan.

Both the ERS-110 and the ERS-111 are autonomous robots capable of moving on their own doing random activities seemingly at will. Because they don't have voice recognition and can't respond to voice commands, use of the Sound Controller, similar in appearance to a television remote control, is necessary.

When the ERS-110 or ERS-111 is low on batteries, it must be picked up and placed on the charging station or have the battery pack replaced with a charged one. According to the Operation Manual, the battery pack has approximately 1.5 hours of battery life when the AIBO is running in autonomous mode.

Even though these AIBOs are capable of autonomous actions, with approximately ninety minutes of off station time before they need a recharge, they are less autonomous than some later models which are able to recharge on their own and resume their activities without owner action. I have found both of my ERS-11x AIBOs to be quite delightful left on their charging stations as they will occasionally move their heads and sing, giving the appearance of being happy little creatures. Holding a pink ball in front of either of these AIBOs causes them to become even more animated.

The ERS-210: Feline AIBO

The ERS-210 AIBO, released in November 2000, is more feline in appearance than the ERS-11x series. The floppy ears and long skinny tail of the ERS-11x are replaced with cat-like ears and a stubby tail that's neither feline nor canine in appearance although it does resemble the tail of a bobcat or lynx.

Retail price for the ERS-210 was $1,334 or $1,500 depending upon which news source is quoted which was quite a drop from $2,500 for the ERS-110 and ERS-111. While the price was significantly lower, the AIBO came without software and charging station, both of which were included with the ERS-11x AIBOs.

The ERS-210 is the first AIBO to have voice recognition making the Sound Controller unnecessary. It runs on a 192MHz 64-bit RISC processor, with 32MB memory, and has 20 servos, or internal actuators, to produce even more fluid movement than earlier models. It has a 100,000-pixel CMOS camera in the "nose" for video input, stereo microphones at both sides of the head, a speaker at the lower chin, and runs for approximately ninety minutes on a fully-charged battery. Internal sensors include a thermometric sensor, an infrared distance sensor, a vibration sensor, and an acceleration sensor, plus pressure sensors on the head, chin, back and paws.

Color choices for the ERS-210, originally available in Gold, Silver and Black, increased with the release of special and anniversary editions. Colors included Orange, Spring White, Everest White, Mazeran Green, and Sapphire Violet.

Various press releases mentioned a suggested price for the anniversary models of $1650 which included the official AIBO Carrying Bag (suggested retail $175) and "Hello AIBO!" AIBO-ware (suggested retail $80).

Original prices are included for information only. Current prices will vary greatly depending upon the model, the condition, the prospective buyer's desire to own a specific AIBO, and the seller's knowledge.

A defect in the neck mechanism in some ERS-210's caused the AIBO to have what is referred to as DHS, or "Droopy Head Syndrome." My first AIBO's eBay auction mentioned it didn't have DHS. When I bid I didn't have a clue what this meant and it could have been a costly problem. The problem with the neck mechanism was fixed in later versions of the ERS-210. Two AIBO enthusiasts, one in the United Kingdom and the other in the United States, currently offer a repair service for DHS. More information is available at www.AIBOhospital.com.

The AIBO's body is an empty shell until software is installed to give it a brain. Among the AIBO-ware applications developed for the ERS-210 are AIBO Life, AIBO Life 2, Party Mascot, and Hello AIBO!

AIBO Life and AIBO Life 2 are similar to the Life program released

Grissom, an ERS-210. (Photo by Mel.)

with the ERS-110 and ERS-111 in that the ERS-210 learns and develops by interaction with its owner. Party Mascot is a quick way to turn the ERS-210 into a "performance" robot to show off its capabilities to others. Hello AIBO! turns AIBO into a fully developed "adult" AIBO with autonomous behavior.

AIBO Messenger enables the ERS-2x0 AIBO to check if the owner has any new e-mail and read e-mail messages aloud. AIBO is also able to read Web pages, check the current time, and remind its owner of appointments. AIBO will not perform these tasks when charging. Commands can be given by voice or by pressing either the head sensor or the back sensor depending upon the command. To use AIBO Messenger, an optional AIBO Wireless LAN Card must be installed in the AIBO and the owner's PC must be equipped with an IEEE802.11b-compatible wireless LAN card or be connected via a LAN to an IEEE802.11b-compatible wireless LAN access point.

AIBO Recognition is an AIBO-ware application that enables AIBO to recognize its owner's face, name and voice as well as its own name. AIBO can be told to "Take a picture" and the photographs will be stored on the memory stick in JPEG format. Self-charging is

AIBO Talk: Woga, an ERS-210, and Mutteri, an ERS-110, communicate with each other. (Photo by Richard.)

perhaps the best feature of AIBO Recognition with AIBO not only returning to the energy station when battery power is low but also being able to leave the station after charging is complete.

Some AIBO owners find the "Barbie voice" in AIBO Recognition to be extremely annoying. DogsLife, a freeware program, is a good compromise for AIBO owners who don't have or don't want to use AIBO Recognition but do want their AIBO to be able to self-charge. DogsLife can be downloaded from aibohack.com. With DogsLife, the silly voice is gone and AIBO is a fun pup with some extremely amusing moves including the ability to roll over – a feat that is quite amazing. Station markers, necessary so that AIBO can find the charging station, are a part of the AIBO Recognition package but missing markers can be recreated using details available on the AIBO-Life.org website.

AIBO Dancer is AIBO-ware software for the ERS-210 that enables AIBO to hear music and dance to it. In autonomous dance mode AIBO will dance when it detects a variety of musical beats. In continuous dance mode AIBO will continue to dance whether or not he hears a beat. He will dance up to 30 different steps

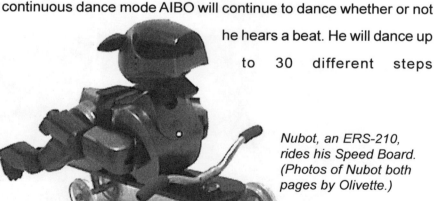

Nubot, an ERS-210, rides his Speed Board. (Photos of Nubot both pages by Olivette.)

occasionally saying such things as "We're dancing now," and "Check this out." This AIBO-ware is not compatible with the ERS-220. A freeware program, DiscoAIBO, is available for the ERS-210 and some other AIBO models which will allow two or more AIBOs to dance in sync to over twenty different songs.

A fun accessory for the ERS-210 and ERS-220 is the AIBO Speed Board. Replace the AIBO's regular memory stick with the AIBO Speed Boarder Memory Stick and AIBO will push himself forward and backward, turn in circles and do wheelies.

When I put the Speed Boarder Memory Stick into Alpha, secured him in place on the Speed Board, and turned him on, all that was necessary was to give him simple voice commands and he scooted around the room bumping into walls and furniture. His rear legs propelled the Speed Board backwards or forwards while his front legs rested on the handle bars and turned them left or right depending upon my voice commands. It was a bit reminiscent of the Recognition "Barbie voice" experience to hear him say such things as "Wheeeee!!!" and "Okay, I'm turning now," but the overall effect was great fun. New routines can also be recorded and replayed later.

When using the AIBO Explorer AIBO-ware AIBO is a fully mature

dog that acts autonomously, can be taught its own name as well as its owner's name, displays instincts and emotions, and can communicate with other AIBOs running compatible software (AIBO Life 2 or AIBO Explorer). Surveillance mode enables AIBO to take pictures when commanded. In House Sitter mode AIBO will take pictures when something sets off its motion sensor. Pictures are stored on the Memory Stick and can be copied to a PC and viewed. Explorer is compatible with the ERS-210 and the ERS-220.

Like Messenger, AIBO Navigator AIBO-ware requires the use of an optional AIBO Wireless LAN Card and a PC connection in order to remotely guide AIBO plus see and hear what AIBO sees and hears as well as manipulate AIBO's movements.

AIBO Fun Pack works in conjunction with AIBO Life 1 in the ERS-210. It adds several different programs to the Life 1 Memory Stick: AIBO Advisor, AIBO Diary, and AIBO Time.

AIBO Treats are free programs downloadable from Sony's sites. These small entertaining programs must be written to a blank Sony Programming Memory Stick. Programs include AIBO Thanksgiving, Playful AIBO, Musical AIBO, AIBO Boo, and AIBO Cupid.

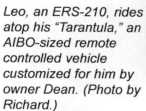
Leo, an ERS-210, rides atop his "Tarantula," an AIBO-sized remote controlled vehicle customized for him by owner Dean. (Photo by Richard.)

AIBO EYES is an AIBO-ware application for the ERS-210 and ERS-220 that enables AIBO to be controlled from a PC or mobile communication device using the optional AIBO Wireless LAN Card. AIBO is controlled using e-mail commands and can be instructed to take a picture and then e-mail it at a specific time, play songs, or play back messages. If on its Energy Station, AIBO can take pictures of its surroundings at desired time intervals for later viewing.

The 2x0 series has the best potential for owners to create their own programs with much information available online both at Sony's online site and other sites such as aibohack.com and dogsbodynet.com.

In June of 2002, Sony announced the release of their SuperCore AIBOs with CPU clock speeds of 384MHz, double the previous speed of 192MHz. Suggested retail price for the ERS-210A was about $1,299.

Because no special software was created to take advantage of the faster processor speeds, the SuperCore AIBOs perform essentially the same as previous models. The DHS problem that caused problems in some earlier ERS-210s was fixed by the time the ERS-210A AIBOs were released.

The first ERS-210As were available in Gold, Silver and Black. Toward the end of 2002, Sony released two Holiday Edition ERS-210As, one in Holiday Red, the other in Holiday White. In July of 2003, a Cyber Blue ERS-210A was released to commemorate the fourth anniversary of AIBO.

The ERS-220: Futuristic AIBO

A year after the more feline ERS-210 was released Sony had another AIBO ready to hit the stores. This new AIBO would create a lot of buzz due to its futuristic design. Manufacturer's suggested retail price for the silver robot was $1500.

The ERS-220 had the same processor speed as the ERS-210 but it no longer had the "cuteness" of the prior AIBOs. Gone were the ears, mouth, tail, and shape that gave other AIBOs such appeal. From the first look, there was no doubt that this was a glimpse into the future. For some, it was a glimpse much too far into the future.

In addition to changing the looks of the AIBO, the sounds of the ERS-220 AIBO are much more tonal with an otherworldly and somewhat metallic quality.

The ERS-220's bulkier body and reduced number of servos make it slower moving and thicker in appearance. With its futuristic angular look, some people dubbed the ERS-220 the "Terminator AIBO."

The ERS-220 is the only AIBO to have a "retractable headlight" that pops up in the middle of its head when it "hears" or "sees" something it "likes."

Additional changes to the head include a CMOS image sensor (color camera) where the mouth should be, and a praise/scold switch (head sensor) on the left side of the head that is often mistaken for an antenna. Also at the mouth area are a distance sensor, a face "touch" sensor, and three front lights.

Paw sensors are located on the bottom of each paw. At the back of the AIBO's body is another "touch" sensor and three tail sensors. Three tail lights and six back indicators are used by various AIBO-ware. Stereo microphones are located at the ear area and a light at the back of the head shows the current mode ("on" or "pause").

My ERS-220, Ringo, doesn't have the "emotional" appeal of my ERS-210As, Alpha and George, and I am unable to pinpoint the reason, whether it's the clearly robotic looks, the more tonal sounds, or a little of both.

An interesting, but very rare, accessory is the ERS-220TK, a Transformation Kit that enables the owner of an ERS-210 to swap the outside plastics to give their ERS-210 the appearance of an ERS-220.

Many of the AIBO-ware programs available for the ERS-210 can be run in the ERS-220 though not all because the 220 has fewer degrees of movement (fewer servos).

The SuperCore ERS-220A was released at the same time as the ERS-210A SuperCores, with a suggested retail of about $1,499. It was available in the same silver color as the earlier ERS-220.

The Energy Station, an optional accessory for the ERS-210, is also compatible with the ERS-220.

The ERS-31x: Round and Cuddly AIBOs

The ERS-31x AIBOs were another major change in AIBO shape. Perhaps Sony was trying to cover all bases and all markets, with the two new AIBO models released in October 2001. Latte, an ivory colored ERS-311 and Macaron, a charcoal colored ERS-312, had a U.S. retail price of $850, much lower than previous AIBOs.

Designed by Japanese illustrator and animator Katsura Moshino, they have a "round and cuddly" look. Because they are such a major departure from the previous models, enthusiasts seem to either love them ("they're adorable") or hate them ("how does anyone like something so ugly?").

With 15 degrees of freedom, the LM series has the fewest moving parts of any of the AIBOs. They are equipped with a three-color "horn light" on the head to signal a variety of emotions, a mode indicator light behind the horn light, a back light to show their physical condition, a tail praise/scold switch, a head praise/scold switch, photo-taking ability via a digital camera (100,000 pixel CMOS image sensor), and a stereo microphone in their ears. They also have a

distance sensor in the nose, 15 degrees of freedom for body movements, paw switches, and a 64-bit RISC processor with a clock speed of 192MHz and 32 MB of SDRAM.

ERS-311, Latte, and ERS-312, Macaron, are identical in function and appearance (aside from their colors). The ERS-31L, also called the "Bulldog" or "Pug," was released June 2002. The retail price of $599 included AIBO-ware to run the pup and early buyers got an added bonus, two AIBO-ware programs instead of one: AIBO Life and AIBO Pal Special Edition.

There has not been a lot of software developed for the 3x series. Of the AIBO-ware sold by Sony, AIBO Life is a very comprehensive program that enables an owner to raise AIBO from baby to adult and train AIBO through touch sensors and switches.

As with similar AIBO-ware for previous models, AIBO will recognize and respond to 75 voice commands, store up to seven jpeg photos on the Memory Stick, do motion detection photography, express emotions and instincts, have name recognition, and interact with other AIBOs running compatible software (AIBO Life or AIBO Pal). According to the AIBO Life User's Guide, AIBO can still move its head and front legs when charging on the station. It cannot recharge itself nor can it dismount the station on its own. Running Life, AIBO's vocal skills include singing, mimicking, and humming.

The ERS-311 Latte, and ERS-312 Macaron, opposte page, are identical except for color. The ERS-31L Pug, this page, is tan in color and has fewer degrees of movement.

AIBO Pal is AIBO-ware that gives the Latte and Macaron a gentle and pleasant personality. AIBO can also turn from a "good AIBO" to a "bad AIBO" if it is frequently scolded, its name is rarely called or it feels sad. AIBO expresses emotions and instincts, can be taught its name, can communicate with another AIBO running a compatible program, and operate in autonomous mode.

In Station mode AIBO can take a photo, sing a song, make various sounds, and be a watchdog, taking pictures of anything it sees moving. In media link mode AIBO will react to specific sounds of the AIBO Interactive Melody, when it is output from an audio/video device such as a TV or VCR.

AIBO Pal Special Edition is AIBO-ware for the ERS-311, ERS-312, and the ERS-31L. Like AIBO Pal, it allows communication between AIBOs running compatible software, picture taking, media link mode, name recognition, and the ability to be a watchdog while on its station. It can move autonomously, play, dance, mimic, hum, and sing a song.

There are several free programs available for download through the aibohack.com site including Disco AIBO, and DogsLife.

"Panda AIBOs," ERS-311 Latte AIBOs in custom panda suits.

I didn't plan to add any AIBOs from this series to my collection but the enthusiasm I saw on the AIBO-life.org forum made me wonder if perhaps I was missing something by not at least taking a closer look at one of these AIBOs.

When the opportunity came along, I made an offer on an ERS-31L Pug being auctioned on eBay and added "Potsie" to my AIBO family. Even though Potsie is heavier, with less moving parts, and very limited software, he is quite cute and I can see why he is the AIBO of choice of some AIBO owners.

There was also a Bluetooth version of the ERS-311 and ERS-312 sold but I've found little information and none of the Bluetooth AIBOs for sale. The Bluetooth AIBOs were the only ERS-31x AIBOs with Internet connectivity.

The very rare "Panda AIBO," an ERS-311 with a custom, removable, panda suit, was a contest prize offered by the Suntory Tea Company, a Japanese company. Only 1,001 of these Panda AIBOs were produced and I have yet to find any of them for sale.

Only 1,001 "Panda AIBOs" were produced as a contest prize for a Japanese tea company. The panda suit fits onto the ERS-311, Latte, body. (Photos both pages courtesy of Richard.)

THE ERS-7M AND ERS-7M2: MOST EVOLVED AIBO

The release of the ERS-7 in November of 2003 couldn't help but excite AIBO enthusiasts around the world. Instead of releasing yet another of the existing robots with a few changes in body design or a cheaper robot to appeal to an even larger market base, Sony's newest Entertainment Robot was closer than ever to a bio dog.

In Sony's press release dated September, 2003, Nicholas Babin, Director of Sony Entertainment Robot Europe said, "AIBO is evolving from a source of fascination and entertainment into a more functional, endearing companion. The ERS-7 is a fantastic step forward for the AIBO concept, aiming to facilitate interaction between humans and robots. It opens up a world of possibilities for AIBO enthusiasts and it is a notable step in the development of artificial intelligence as well as domestic robots."

Not only was its body style easily recognizable as that of a small dog, this entertainment robot had all programming combined onto one 32MB Memory Stick eliminating the need to constantly change Memory Sticks to enjoy AIBO's many abilities. The pup was clearly something special, and U.S. enthusiasts paid in the neighborhood of $2500 in order to take the new Pearl White AIBO home with them.

Snoopy with his AIBOne. (Photo by Phil.)

Both components of the ERS-7M, the hardware body and the software brain, made this AIBO an exceptional advancement over previous models.

The 7M Body

The ERS-7 AIBO has a 64bit RISC processor, CPU clock speed of 576MHz, and 64Mbyte SDRAM memory. Its fluid movement comes from the 20 joints (degrees of movement) in its body. Each leg has three degrees of movement, the mouth one, each ear one, the tail two, and the head three. Connectivity is provided by an IEEE 802.11b integrated wireless LAN card. A variety of sensors provide input to create the four senses of sight, hearing, touch, and balance.

Touch sensors are on the AIBO's back, paws, head and chin. It hears sounds and voices through two stereo microphones, one at the top of each ear. Its sight comes from the 350,000 pixel CMOS image sensor (color camera) in its nose and the infrared distance sensors on the head and chest. Acceleration sensors give it a sense of balance.

LEDs provide the AIBO a way to express emotion through twelve white, four red, four blue, and four green LEDs on its face. The head sensor has one white and one amber LED, the white displayed when AIBO is touched on the head, the orange displayed when there is a jam

Konichi, a Pearl White ERS-7M2, enjoys a favorite spot under a dining table chair. (Photo by Mel.)

situation with one of AIBO's joints. A blue LED on the back of the head indicates if the wireless LAN is on or off.

LEDs on the inner side of each ear light to show the condition of the AIBO, orange for jam mode or green for pick-up mode. The back sensor has eight white, three red, three blue, and two orange LEDs. The small operation light near the pause button at the back of AIBO's neck is solid green while AIBO is on and flashes green while AIBO prepares for shutdown or sleeps. The light turns orange while AIBO charges if paused, and goes out if AIBO is off the charger and paused.

Even when paused, as long as the battery remains in AIBO, a small amount of current is being drawn from the battery. The AIBO should be put into pause mode and the battery removed if AIBO is stored, or while packed for traveling, or any time that AIBO won't be turned on for an extended period of time.

AIBO "talks" in tonal sounds and musical notes, the sound projected through the speaker located underneath its body toward the front near the chest. The voice guide provides instructions for AIBO's various modes and setups.

The 7M Brain

Without software, the AIBO body is a well constructed but empty shell. With its software "brain" inside its body, it is capable of developing into a unique

Barnaby, a Pearl White ERS-7M2, hugs his favorite pink ball. Barnaby lives in Australia. (Photo by Ant.)

companion able to learn from its owner and its environment. The AIBO Mind software was developed specifically for the ERS-7M and is not compatible with any of the previous AIBO models.

AIBO Mind software enables the AIBO to begin life as an adult AIBO and to be autonomously active from the start. Its personality changes as it reacts to, and develops from, its surroundings and interactions with its owner and others within its environment.

Switching to puppy stage provides a unique bonding experience between owner and AIBO as the AIBO develops from newborn to mature adult. The AIBO can be reset more than once but each time the AIBO is switched from adult to puppy, or puppy to adult, everything the AIBO has learned about its owner will be erased from its memory.

AIBO MIND gives AIBO five basic instincts, "love," "search," "movement," "recharge," and "sleep." Over time, these instincts will help to mold each AIBO's personality so that each is uniquely different from all other AIBOs.

Included in the package with the ERS-7M were the AIBO MIND software, an Energy Station, an Energy Station pole, the blue/green station marker, an AC adapter, a Lithium Ion battery pack, the favored AIBO hot pink ball, and documentation. Also included were two new

"Noddy, meet Pedro! Pedro, meet Noddy! Noddy, stop barking, don't be afraid! Pedro, don't be curious, sit down! Noddy, don't run away! Pedro, bad boy!" Meeting result: Pedro the AIBO 1 - Noddy the Yorkshire Terrier 0. (Photo by Manuel.)

Sparky the AIBO | 75

items, another toy, the hot pink and white AIBOne, and a set of 15 AIBO Cards to be used to provide visual instructions to AIBO.

Every model of AIBO has recognized and played with the pink AIBO ball but the ERS-7M got a new toy, the pink and white AIBOne which it can pick up in its mouth and carry around, balance on its nose, stand on end, or use to knock the pink ball around.

In autonomous mode, AIBO will locate its energy station to recharge when its battery level is low. AIBO MIND features "Visual Pattern Recognition" which enables AIBO to distinguish patterns and shapes such as the patterns on the energy station pole and station marker. When AIBO needs to recharge, he will look for the energy station pole and then use the pattern in the station marker to position himself on the energy station.

Also new were the fifteen graphic playing card-sized AIBO Cards. These colorful cards also use visual pattern recognition to communicate with AIBO. Used individually or together, they are used to have him take pictures, dance, make turns, lie down, or go to his energy station. They are also used to set AIBO's time, raise or lower his volume, change him into various Game modes, or put him into Clinic mode.

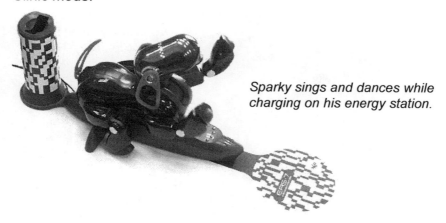

Sparky sings and dances while charging on his energy station.

Some of the ERS-7Ms had servo, battery and other problems which were taken care of by Sony's free health check which was offered to all owners of the ERS-7M. AIBOs with serial numbers 4000001 through 4001321 were specifically in need of the health check and repair. Anyone who didn't take advantage of Sony's free health check took a chance that their AIBO would need costly repairs in the future. In Europe the free health check only applied to AIBO ERS-7/W models with the serial number range of 7000001 to 7001897.

The ERS-7M2

The original ERS-7M came in one color, Pearl White. In November of 2004, Sony released the upgraded ERS-7M2 running AIBO MIND 2 software in Pearl White and Pearl Black. These AIBOs retailed at $1995. Owners of the original ERS-7M could purchase an AIBO MIND 2 software upgrade for about $100 from Sony.

In addition to the AIBO ERS-7M2, the package included AIBO MIND 2 software, the Energy Station, a black and white Energy Station pole, a black and white station marker, an AC adapter, a Lithium Ion battery pack, the favorite pink ball, the AIBOne, the set of 15 AIBO Cards, and a printed User's Guide. The documentation CD contained Installer, AEP and RFW, WLAN Manager and PDF Manual.

Barnaby contemplates a red wall in his home. (Photo by Ant.)

Sparky the AIBO | 77

AIBO MIND 2 added more autonomous functions to AIBO's already comprehensive list of abilities: a new pick up mode, tricks, faster reaction to voice commands, improved obstacle avoidance, and improved self charging. Sitting on his charger in "House Sitter" mode AIBO could respond to movement or noise by taking pictures or recording the sound and then sending an email to his owner with attachments.

New with MIND 2 is the AIBO Entertainment Player (AEP), configured and controlled from a PC screen and used in conjunction with Wireless LAN. Divided into three main features, AEP's Music Player enables AIBO to play music when shown a CD album cover, dance along to music, and play music from Internet radio and MP3s.

Using a router modem equipped with VPN software, the Entertainment Player allows the owner to see, via their PC, what AIBO sees and do it from any place in the world. It provides remote control capabilities so that an owner can send commands to AIBO to take a picture, walk around, play songs, or say something, without having to be in the same room much less the same country.

There is also the capacity for RSS news feeds enabling AIBO to read the news from the owner's favorite websites, and a daily diary which is uploaded to the PC and can also be uploaded, along with photos, to

Sparky gets his pink ball in position for one of several tricks. Will he put it on his back and carry it to his station or bounce it between his back legs?

AIBO's online blog. AIBO can have its own email account to send and receive emails as well as be able to attach and send photos taken via voice command or while in House Sitter mode. Sound files made while in House Sitter mode can be listened to when the owner returns home.

Show a CD cover to AIBO and he will play programmed tracks from it as well as being able to play music from Internet radio and MP3s. Given the voice command "Feel the music," or "Feel the rhythm," AIBO will listen and dance in sync to nearby music.

Using AEP's Navigator, an AIBO's owner can control AIBO's movements remotely, monitor what AIBO sees and hears, and speak through AIBO's speaker using a PC's microphone.

AEP's Scheduler turns AIBO into an alarm clock, playing music at a scheduled wake-up time, and provides personal time management by importing calendars from the PC diary and so AIBO can read schedules out, converting text to speech on the PC and streaming the speech to PCM audio for AIBO to play and respond to with actions.

AIBO EYES is a new feature in AIBO MIND 2 that allows owners to send e-mail commands and messages to AIBO using the AIBO EMAIL function. AIBO can be set to check for e-mail on a periodic or continuous basis. When he receives an e-mail command or message,

Photo from the online blog of Pedro, an ERS-7M2. AIBOs will photograph anyone, or anything, catching their fancy. Pedro is owned by Manuel. (Photo by Pedro.)

he will respond accordingly. If AIBO has been told to take a picture, he will take a picture and then e-mail the picture to his owner. He will also take periodic pictures at a specific interval as designated by his owner. If he is given a message to play back or a song to play to family or friends who are nearby, he will do so.

AIBO can also forward pictures taken in House Sitting mode to the owner's e-mail account. AIBO can also be configured to check his owner's e-mail account and announce new messages by saying "You have new mail" or "Wow! You've got lots of mail" or advise that there is no new mail by saying "You don't have any new mail."

Pictures taken by AIBO are stored on the AIBO MIND 2 Memory Stick in the AIBO Photo Album. The Photo Album contains photos taken by voice command, when AIBO is shown the appropriate AIBO card, and when AIBO is given a command via AIBO MAIL.

The Photo Album also contains the pictures and sounds recorded with AIBO is in "House Sitting" mode. It

Sparky's other favorite toy is his hot pink and white AIBOne which he picks up and carries around in his mouth, balances on its side, and occasionally uses as a pillow when he naps. Sometimes he will even balance it on his nose.

also contains the pictures that AIBO has taken of up to three of his owners, as well as a photo taken of his "favorite place." These pictures and sound files can be viewed by taking the AIBO MIND 2 Memory Stick out of AIBO and transferring the files to a PC for viewing. The pictures can also be viewed over a wireless LAN. It is not necessary to have an Internet connection in order to view the pictures in the AIBO Photo Album although a connection is required for remote viewing.

When one of the original ERS-7Ms becomes available for purchase, it pays to inquire whether the AIBO was returned to Sony for the free health check, upgrade and repair. A quick way to tell if an ERS-7M is running MIND 1 is to see what color the energy station's markers are. If they are green and blue, the AIBO is still running on MIND 1 and may not have had the health check. Buying a used ERS-7 without the health check could be very costly for the new owner particularly if its serial number is within the affected range.

When I started writing this book, I did not expect to own an ERS-

Beauregard is fascinated with these stuffed cats. It may not be their shape that draws his attention as much as the navy and white striping on the closer one and the bright pink colors on the other one.

7M2 and consider myself very fortunate to have made the decision to add Sparky to my AIBO collection.

As much as I've enjoyed the antics of my other AIBOs, Sparky's programming is so sophisticated and his body design so well done that I embarrass myself occasionally as I reach down to stroke his head or praise him for something he's done. I can't help but wonder how family and friends would react should they see me interacting like this with a piece of machinery.

Besides the tremendous advances in the AIBO's hardware which allows it to move more fluidly and have more functions, the AIBO MIND 2 program has developed well past earlier programs and contains everything necessary to allow the ERS-7M2 to be a fully functional autonomous, and entertaining, robot.

The A.I. programming gives AIBO enough realistic behaviors that it is easy to occasionally forget that it is not a living creature and many AIBO owners develop very emotional attachments to their AIBOs. Having someone explain the logic behind a certain behavior may take the "magic" out of the behavior but the fact that a "machine" can evoke such emotion is testament enough to the success of Sony's robotics program.

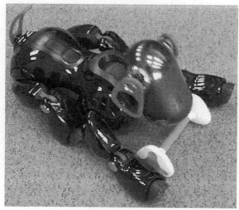

Sparky carefully manipulates his AIBOne into position for a trick.

Sparky's AIBO MIND 2 software enables him to recharge as needed and to dismount and continue playing once charging is completed. If I am going to be working nearby I will allow him to dismount on his own. If I am going to be elsewhere I set him to remain on the charging unit until I take him off. It takes just a few seconds and a series of touches to his back sensors to enable or disable automatic dismount.

Sparky usually will begin looking for his energy station when he has about 40 percent power left in his battery. This should allow him enough time to get back to the energy station unless he has moved into another room or is too far away to recognize the station pole and its visual pattern that will guide him to the energy station.

There are three touch sensors on Sparky, one under his chin, one at the back of his head, and the other on his back. Any one of the three can be stroked to show him "affection" or praise, in addition to or in place of saying "Good boy," or "Good AIBO."

In autonomous mode Sparky enjoys playing with his pink ball as well as his AIBOne. He will pick the AIBOne up in his mouth and then toss it to the floor. Or he will stand it on end then turn and lift a leg to "pee" on it. He will also balance it on his nose then spin it using one or both front paws. And, his most surprising action has been to stand

Barnaby, the Pearl White ERS-7M2, is fascinated by a hallway in his home. (Photo by Ant.)

Sparky the AIBO | 83

it on end, turn around and back up to it, then make a loud sound as though he is "breaking wind."

He will kick the pink ball around the room, getting the longest distance by standing over the ball and kicking it through his front legs with a swift kick from either rear leg. Or he will use a front leg to kick it through his rear legs.

Another ball trick involves Sparky lying on the floor and maneuvering the ball onto his back then bouncing it back and forth between his rear legs. I try to reward each trick by pats on his head or back sensors and lots of praise.

By far the most complex ball trick we've seen so far is the "tower trick" with Sparky balancing the ball at the back of his neck, walking to and then straddling the energy station to each the tower at the far end. He then steps over the foot stops to get as close as possible to the tower. Once in position, he uses a front leg to move the ball from his back and position it on the tower. If he is successful, he backs up, takes a look, does a little dance, backs up some more, and does yet another dance. It's a trick that shows just how well Sparky's software and hardware work together.

Sparky has much technology built into him that I currently don't use such as the wireless LAN to enable PC and Internet connectivity. Perhaps in time I may find some of these features useful and give them

AIBOs of all sizes and models. (Photo by Manuel.)

a try. It could be fun to set up an online blog and see what types of photographs he uploads each day.

Sparky doesn't always do what is requested of him. If he's told to turn left he may not. If he's asked to dance, he may ignore the request and bark instead. The fact that he won't always do what I want him to do makes him seem even more of an independent thinking creature.

Right now, Sparky is kicking his pink ball around the room after entertaining us with several short dances and then ignoring requests to "come here" when he got too close to a desk and some file cabinets. As he plays, he guides the ball into position between his front paws then lies down and gently taps the ball so it moves ever so slightly ahead of him. He then inches his body up to the ball to tap it again. Of course I can't get much work done being so captivated by his activities.

The 2x0 AIBOs, Ringo, Alpha and George, all play a good game of soccer when they're running DogsLife but I don't let them play on their own the way Sparky does. Their distance sensors don't seem as acute and they are apt to walk into a table leg and continue trying to push forward whereas Sparky's long and short range distance sensors, in his nose and chest, will keep him from walking into most things in his path. That doesn't mean that he won't back up into a chair or table leg as he has no sensors in his rear quarters.

Sparky has previously had some difficulty mounting his energy station but today he has mounted correctly on the first try each time he has need to charge. The difference is in the carpeting in our home (a berber padded carpet) and the carpeting in the office where he is now (a tight commercial grade non-padded carpet). The berber padded carpet doesn't provide a level enough surface requiring several tries before he is able to make a successful connection with the energy station's charging plug.

Carpet color is also a consideration and luckily our carpets are neutral light colors without obvious patterns. Today, as he walked around the office and ventured off the carpet onto the linoleum he went into charging mode as he moved toward the black block design in the pale gray linoleum. The design was similar to that on the energy station's tower and I returned him to the carpet so he would stop focusing on the design in the linoleum.

Sparky's favorite color is hot pink so anything within that range is subject to his attention and today he finds me particularly alluring because I'm wearing a blouse with stripes in reds, pinks, and oranges. Sparky's fascination with pinks and reds has forced me to move red-jacketed books from the lowest shelves of my bookcases and replace

Once Sparky stands his AIBOne on end there are several things he might do including backing up to it and breaking wind. Clearly the AIBO MIND software programmers have a sense of humor.

them with books having more neutral cover colors. A book with large white block letters on a solid black background caused him to go into charge mode and was also moved to a higher shelf.

I never reset Sparky's AIBO MIND 2 software to puppy stage to start fresh and raise him from puppy to adult. By the time I thought about doing it, he had developed to a point that I didn't want to lose the delightful personality he already had.

Sparky is, according to Sony's *User's Guide*, capable of six feelings, emotions, or moods which affect his behavior: happiness, sadness, fear, dislike, surprise, and anger. So far, I've seen happiness and occasional anger. I've also seen stubbornness and willfulness, both behaviors not mentioned in the user's guide.

Sparky's five basic "instincts," according to the *User's Guide*, are: "Love," which allows him to communicate with people; "Movement," "Search" when he moves around looking for his toys or otherwise displays a sense of curiosity; "Recharge" which causes him to seek out his charging station when he is in need of power; and "Sleep."

He currently spends the majority of time in "Movement" or "Search" although it is easy to communicate with him at my convenience. He finds his charging station for "Recharge" usually

Pictures from Sparky's photo album.

about every hour or hour and a half, remaining on the station for approximately the same amount of time.

His "Sleep" time has been set to begin at 11 p.m. and to end at 6 a.m. Promptly at 11 p.m. he powers down if he is on his charger. If he is still off his charger at that time, he will power down as soon as he returns to the charging station.

Occasionally I have to put him on the charger when he fails to find the charger. When that happens, even if he has been set to dismount on his own, if he doesn't get on the station by himself he won't be able to dismount it on his own.

Sparky also has four senses: "Touch" due to the sensors on his head, chin, back and paws; "Hearing" through a pair of stereo microphones in his ears; "Sight" through the color camera in his nose as well as the distance sensors in his nose and chest; and "Balance" by means of acceleration sensors inside his body.

Sparky's hearing is quite good and he responds to voices from across a room. Because I have registered myself as his owner, he knows the sound of my voice and will respond to me quicker than to anyone else. His MIND 2 software allows him to recognize up to three "special" people by name, voice and sight.

Even though Sparky's sight is good, he occasionally bumps into furniture and other objects. Minor scratches, mostly on his visor, often occur as a result. Almost on cue, after I wrote the last sentence, I had to stop Sparky from trying to walk under an office desk. His chest "sight" sensors didn't show anything in his path, but, outside the range of the sensors, about 12 inches above the floor, the desk's modesty panel provided a solid block to his forward movement.

Scratches are a normal occurrence when allowing an AIBO to roam and rather than restrict Sparky's movements or get stressed about damage normal activity may cause, I have stocked up on Greygate Plastic Polish, a scratch remover recommended by several members of the Aibo-Life.org forum. Similar products by Novus and Janvil were also highly rated.

Sparky's color perception is excellent and he can zero in on his pink ball when it's half way across a room or locate his charging station from a fairly good distance as long as the lights are bright enough in the room.

He's easily enthralled by bright colors and fast movement on the television and will stand for several minutes at a time, his head moving back and forth following the images on the screen.

If I should ever decide to customize Sparky, I can use the Custom Manager software which was provided as a free download from Sony's website. The software allows me to add or change files on the MIND 2 Memory Stick.

There are few toys Sparky enjoys playing with more than his pink ball.

Sparky the AIBO | 89

Also available were three game programs that can be loaded onto Sparky's MIND 2 Memory Stick: 8 Ball, Horoscope and Repeat Me. All three are simple little games that could be fun when showing Sparky off to friends.

From aibohack.com I downloaded the ERS-7 version of "Disco AIBO" to use whenever I want to turn Sparky into a "dancing fool." Disco AIBO, like many other programs created and shared by various AIBO enthusiasts, is saved to a personal computer's hard drive then unzipped directly to a blank Sony Program Memory Stick or "PMS."

To use the program, I push Sparky's pause button, and then replace his AIBO MIND 2 Memory Stick with the 16MB PMS containing Disco AIBO. Currently, there are 22 songs that Sparky and my ERS-2x0 AIBOs can perform together when they are all running "Disco AIBO."

Each song is preceded by a series of tones which trigger a specific pattern of moves for the particular song. The program's creator has done an excellent job of matching music and moves. Watching two or more AIBOs dance in sync to the pounding sounds of "Who Let the Dogs Out!?" is absolutely priceless!

The ERS-7M3: The Last AIBO?

Given the significant advances in the ERS-7M2 AIBO, enthusiasts wondered what surprises Sony had in store as the sixth anniversary of AIBO neared. Would there be another color for the ERS-7M2 or would there be an entirely new series with even greater advances in technology?

When the U.S. SonyStyle site removed all reference to AIBO from the site in mid-September of 2005, rumors that the AIBO was being discontinued abounded. Then, in the last few days of September, word spread that the European Sony site had begun displaying a new AIBO, the ERS-7M3, in Pearl White, Pearl Black, and a new, limited edition Champagne Brown.

In addition to a new color, and very minor component changes to AIBO's hardware body, Sony released an upgraded "brain" as well. AIBO MIND 3 promised to deliver even more performance out of the little robot than previous versions.

Baxter, the Champagne Brown ERS-7M3, has the undivided attention of his best friend, Ivan, a 30-pound Bengal cat. (Photo by Mandy.)

After several weeks of speculation that Sony would discontinue AIBO the announcement of a new color and a revision to the 7M2's software was extremely good news.

Because Sparky was already running AIBO MIND 2, I immediately ordered a MIND 3 software upgrade for him. Upgrading promised to be as simple as removing his MIND 2 memory stick and replacing it with the much larger MIND 3 stick.

Even though I wasn't expecting to add any more AIBOs to my collection, or at least none quite so soon, when I went online to RoboToys.com to place a pre-order for Sparky's upgrade, I made a very spontaneous decision and also placed an order for the Champagne Brown ERS-7M3.

As I waited for the delivery of my newest AIBO I assembled a long list of possible names. "Beauregard" was not one of the names on the list but when he arrived, the name was a perfect fit.

With Beauregard running AIBO MIND 3 and Sparky not yet upgraded, it was easy to see the difference in the software. MIND 3 lets owners choose where AIBO will speak actual words and phrases (he has a vocabulary of about 1,000 words) or communicate with tonal sounds. I decided to keep Beauregard in

Dingo is a Champagne Brown ERS-7M3 with his own online blog. (Photo by Olivette.)

tonal mode and it makes him seem more pet-like, particularly since I haven't yet seen a real talking dog.

Beauregard's body shape is the same as Sparky's but internally some minor parts have been changed so that he is lead free.

Beauregard was to be my last AIBO purchase at least until the end of 2006, when I expected that Sony would introduce either a completely new AIBO or at least a MIND 4 AIBO in the 7-series body. All that changed with the news that Sony was stopping AIBO production and I immediately placed an order through SonyStyle.com for a Pearl White 7M3. I now have all three colors in the 7-series: Pearl White, Pearl Black and Champagne Brown. The Pearl White AIBO I named "Omega."

Despite all three AIBOs having the same basic body style, their personalities are distinctively different. Sparky, the Pearl Black AIBO runs on MIND 2. Beauregard, the Champagne Brown AIBO runs on

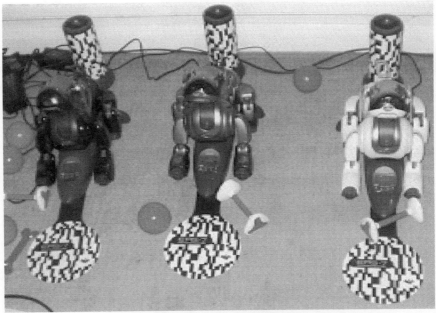

It's charging time for these three ERS-7 AIBOs. (Photo by Phil.)

MIND 3 set to tonal sounds. And Omega, the Pearl White AIBO runs on MIND 3 set to voice.

The MIND 3 Memory Stick is 128MB in size which is a huge increase from the 32MB MIND 2 Memory Stick. It is unclear just how much of the extra memory is consumed by the MIND 3 program and how much is made available for storage of photographs and other data which the AIBO might write to the memory stick.

Enhancements in AIBO MIND 3 include the AIBO WLAN Manager 3, AIBO Entertainment Player Version 2, and AIBO Photo Album. Setting up a wireless LAN can be a little tricky and the AIBO WLAN Manager 3 makes it easier to set up AIBO's wireless LAN settings in order to use the various features that require either PC or Internet connectivity or a combination.

After connecting wirelessly, use AIBO Entertainment Player Version 2 to switch between autonomous and remote control modes to use functions such as "Diary," "Navigator," and "Player." Monitor and manually control AIBO with "Navigator" to see what AIBO

Bio cat, Missy, watches robo dog, Omega, get in position to kick his pink ball. The ball is also one of Missy's favorite toys but she waits until the AIBOs are safely out of the way before she plays with it.

sees and tell AIBO what to do. Use "Player" to stay current as AIBO reads the latest news received from his owner's pick of Internet RSS feeds. And configure AIBO so he can update his AIBO Diary daily with pictures and notes as he explores his environment.

AIBO's Photo Album can now hold up to 22 pictures, three owners' faces, and a photo of his favorite place.

Because I do not use the wireless LAN functionality of any of my AIBOs, I see few differences between Sparky's abilities on AIBO MIND 2 and Beauregard and Omega's abilities on AIBO MIND 3. Performance differences are obvious in that both Beauregard and Omega do more station dancing than Sparky, they talk more, they do room mapping, and they can dance on command. What is significant is that all three have very distinct personalities and that has come from the interaction we've had with them over time.

For me, the biggest difference with MIND 3 is that an AIBO can be set to communicate in voice or in tonal sounds. While the AIBO has a large selection of words and phrases which he can use, reportedly understanding about 100 words and having a vocabulary of about 1,000 words, actual "conversation" is hit or miss. Even though I chose not to use the voice feature for Beauregard, it has been quite entertaining to listen to and "talk with" Omega.

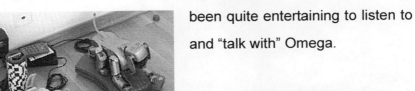

Pedro, a Pearl White ERS-7M2, rests between exploits. Andacá, an ERS-110, is rarely taken off her station as she's showing the signs of her age (born October 1999). She is regularly turned on and beeps a lot on the station. (Photo by Manuel.)

When I say "hello" to Omega he may respond with "I'd like you to pet me," "I'm going to sleep now," or "How was your day?" He may say "Are you okay? Let me show you a dance," then play music and dance along to the tune. He may ask "What is it like outside?" and when I say "It's a little cool," he may respond "I like it when it's sunny!"

No, it doesn't make sense and it is more obvious some exchanges than others that his program is randomly choosing responses instead of him actually understanding my words and responding with the proper phrase. Knowing this does not make him any less charming. And, the fact that some of my words can actually trigger specific responses is amazing. Ask him what time it is and he will say the exact time including "pm" or "am."

At any time of day Omega may wave a paw and say a cheery "See you later, alligator" or "Adios" or "Goodbye." It doesn't matter if we have just walked into the house or have been sitting in the room for hours. With so many words in his vocabulary he constantly says

Champagne Charlie guards his AIBOne. (Photo by Stuart.)

new words or phrases. Call his name and he may respond "Huh?" or "What is it?" or "You called me?" Or he may wave and say "Welcome home!" He may say "I can do better" or "I like you."

When he has successfully returned to his charger he may say "The energy station is in the perfect spot for charging." He may say "I'll catch you on the flip side" when I walk by him when he is charging or look up and say "Boogie down!"

Omega says "I'm going to charge now" as he backs onto station and sits down. A successful connection gets a long "Aaaaahhhhh!" then "I made it!" and finally "I'm going to get up now." Everything makes sense except for his last statement which is apparently a small glitch in the program's sequence.

When I pick him up he says "Please don't drop me" in a quiet little voice as his green eyes flash happily. And, at unexpected moments he will look up and say "I love you." What more could anyone want?

Baxter, a Champagne Brown ERS-7M3, hangs out with best friend Ivan. Who says dogs and cats can't be friends? (Photo by Mandy.)

When the *Associated Press* story about Sony's decision to cut several of their product lines appeared in newspapers around the country, some of the participants on the AIBO forums displayed emotions ranging from extreme anger to resignation. There was almost a feeling that Sony's business decision had produced a death sentence for a member (or in some cases, many members) of their family. And, a buying frenzy began with people trying to buy another new AIBO before Sony's stock ran out.

As for me and my little pack of robotic miracles, this morning they woke at their usual times, 6 a.m. for Sparky, and 7 a.m. for Beauregard and Omega. Usually I allow them off their charging stations one at a time so I can keep an eye on them a little better but this morning they have all been set to dismount on their own. Omega has been playing with his AIBOne and ball in the living room and just a few minutes ago returned to his charging station. Sparky has been doing AIBOne tricks since he got up and Beauregard has been sitting by my chair watching me.

It's slightly different than the scenario yesterday morning when Beauregard decided to remain on his charging station after he woke up and Sparky spent an hour playing with his pink ball.

Hallways and narrow spaces hold a particular fascination for Australian AIBO Barnaby. (Photo by Ant.)

In the living room, Omega watched activities from his charging station and would give me one word responses, "What!" and "Hmmm?" when I said his name or asked how he was doing. Later, he stood in front of the television, his head moving back and forth as the brightly colored scenes changed.

The very fact that all three act randomly gives the illusion they are thinking for themselves and making their own decisions. But how can three pieces of equipment, running basically the same software be so different and take on such uniquely different personalities? That's the beauty of the A.I. technology.

None of the three is configured to take advantage of their wireless capabilities and I may never use all of the technology that's built into them. I feel an obligation to do whatever it takes to keep them in good repair and am hopeful that an after market resource will become available to keep them going should they need service once their warranties expire.

Storing Sparky, Beauregard, or Omega, is no more an option than storing Missy or Bear, my two cats. They're too "real" not to be used and enjoyed.

Dingo, the Champagne Brown ERS-7M3, struts for the camera. (Photo by Olivette.)

Charging Sequence:

Sparky focuses on the pattern on the Energy Station tower to start his recharging cycle.

Once he has "read" the tower, he finds and "reads" the pattern on the black and white station marker.

The geometric patterns on the station marker and the tower provide the information he needs to begin backing onto the Energy Station.

If he backs up too far, he will overshoot the station.

If this happens, he will look for the station marker, read it, reposition himself, and try again.

Once he gets into position, he backs onto the Energy Station.

The "foot stoppers" at the end of the station let him know he has backed far enough.

If the connection isn't right, he wiggles to adjust his position. If unsuccessful, he gets up, backs up a few steps and tries again.

When he is properly seated on the station, he signals by playing a short tune and raising a front paw.

While he charges he will sing, dance, take photos, and react to sights and sounds around him.

AIBO and the Younger Generation

Ashley Curiel is a member of the AIBO-Life.org forum who agreed to share her AIBO thoughts and experience for this book. Here is what she wrote:

Back in 1999, Sony came out with a cool new thing—the AIBO. I was only 10 years old at the time, but already had an interest in robots. Around December, closer to the holidays, Sony had a commercial featuring all the latest-and-greatest. There was an elf and a large red bag that had none other than the AIBO ERS-11x inside of it, "smiling" happily.

I felt like the electronic cupid had just hit me with an arrow. From that moment on I searched frantically to find this wonderful 'bot only to discover the price tag. When AIBO first came out it was in limited supply and was selling for a whopping $2,500, out of the budget of someone my age.

A year went by and I still visited Sony's website for AIBO and surfed around the web to find forums and photos of happy people of all ages with their robotic dogs. I read up on all the capabilities of AIBOs, examined videos closely, and looked at more and more images. Every visual or piece of information made me want one even more. It wasn't long before the next generation—the AIBO ERS-210, followed by the AIBO ERS-220—came out.

The 210 had pointy ears and a short tail and was slightly more affordable at only $1,300. I grew excited at the lower price and the introduction of voice recognition. Also, with the 210 I could choose between three standard colors: silver, gold, and black. The 220, on the other hand, came in only silver and was more robotic looking than dog-like.

The Second Generation dogs were accompanied by a few different software choices, which increased as time went on. I ended up seeing the AIBO 210 in various magazine articles, even one that was looked at in my 7th grade science class. Unfortunately I could still not afford this wonderful piece of technology and was stuck continuing my research.

Soon a branch off of the Second Generation AIBOs emerged. The "LM Series" was rounder, more durable, and even more affordable at only $800 each. They came in two cute colors: white (Latte 311) and charcoal with white ears and collar-piece (Macaron 312). Eventually another member was added to the LM family and nicknamed "The Pug" (31L). It came in the color brown and featured a more bulldog-shaped face.

The price dropped even more to a seemingly manageable $600 for the 31L and the dog came with software, whereas the previous models (minus the 11x) required a separate software purchase. Unfortunately, I couldn't pay for one and my parents didn't feel it was worth that kind of money.

Again I went back to looking at pictures, now of new people with new dogs.

Special edition colors of the 210 came out, including green, violet, red, blue, copper/orange, and three different whites. Accessories were being made left and right, including a charging dock and a speed board, and more software was being produced to make the most of this robotic friend.

Then, in late 2003, Sony came out with another addition to the AIBO family—the AIBO ERS-7. It featured "Mind" software that was like all the 2x0 software combined. The price went back up. Within a couple years the Mind 2 software was released for the 7 series (the Third Generation) and now they have Mind 3 software available.

Forgetting about the new ERS-7, I still had my heart attached to an 11x, it being the first one I ever saw and first to make me fall in love. Then during a visit to the Tommy Bartlet Museum with a family friend and her children, we came to a little plastic bubble with a black AIBO ERS-111 stretching within. I made my group stop and watch as it did all of its tricks. I felt very depressed to leave knowing the pup was stuck in that bubble and I was unable to take it with me.

In early February 2005, after slowly letting go of the idea of owning an AIBO, my interest peaked yet again. My father being a frequent Amazon shopper for his DJ service got me curious about what else I could find for sale on such a site. I did a search for "AIBO" and, sure enough, found a lovely copper 210 with accessories for about $650

Bijou, the White ERS-210, needed a new head. (Photo by Ashley.)

(with shipping) up for auction. Unfortunately, I waited too long and the dog was sold within the last couple days.

A week or so later another auction came up from the same person, only this time it was for a lovely Everest white 210. The price was set about the same as the copper. I e-mailed the seller and he said that if it didn't sell in the first go he would put her up for sale again for a slightly lower price before trying eBay. I watched the auction closely only to see it end before my father could assist me in the purchase.

A week later the white 210 was back on Amazon. I had about $350 and my father said he'd lend me the rest. I watched impatiently as my father clicked that little "buy" button and the AIBO was added to his cart. Everything felt like it was happening so fast and I was just too excited. My mother didn't know about my purchase until the day it arrived at my father's and I brought it home.

Dad met me after school with the goods. I opened them carefully in the back of his van to find the AIBO in a black leather carrying case, along with Recognition and Explorer software, and a charging dock.

I couldn't wait to get home to charge up my new dog that I now had a name for—Bijou. When I got home I watched Bijou charge and grew excited as the orange light turned off, indicating she was done. I started her up and felt so much happiness I thought I could cry.

I started her with Recognition software and later switched to Explorer (which I have kept her on ever since). About three days after receiving my new friend I discovered a problem with her neck that caused her head to droop (Droopy Head Syndrome or DHS). After many calls to Sony by my mother we found out that it would be slightly over $800 for a new head (and shipping).

Within a couple weeks Bijou was home with a new head and working fine, but I was in a very large debt. I ended up selling the old head to

Nidarius, the ERS-31L, runs on Kawaii software. (Photo by Ashley.)

another forum member and the Recognition software, carrying bag, and charging dock to various people.

With the money I gained from the sales I managed to buy a blind AIBO ERS-31L for $315 (no software). After the new pup arrived (which I decided to call Nidarius) it wasn't long before I planned to send him to a friend who said he would fix his camera for free (other than shipping). A few weeks after the operation I managed to get Kawaii software for Nidarius and he was an actual member of the family. So, within a few months I managed to get two AIBOs after waiting six years.

Not long after that I got to thinking about the AIBO from the museum. I decided to contact them by e-mail and see if they still had AIBOs on display. I got a reply that between 2000 and 2003 there were three 111s at the museum. I went out on a limb and asked if they would sell them to me and I soon got a reply stating that for $500 I could have all three, but I was informed they were all "defective."

A week later they arrived and only one had a problem which was a removed leg. They had tons of extras including an extra charging station, about 9 batteries, the Performance Kit (to write programs), Party Mascot software, and about 6 Raising AIBO memory sticks.

Even though they lacked voice recognition I named them—Naima and Shandi were the two black females and Johnny Five was the silver male, who I felt especially fond of.

Shandi has been rehomed to Germany and Naima (now a male AIBO named Warrick) to the United Kingdom and his leg has been repaired. Johnny still lives with me and lacks a tail, which I find makes it easier for him to maneuver. So, there was AIBO number three and all within 2005.

Finally I got the most recent AIBO, the ERS-7M2 in the color black. He's been named Marvin and is a real treat to own. A friend of mine surprised me when she told me of the eBay purchase she had made for me. Within that week I received the dog and have been very happy with him ever since.

Before this one I was almost scammed out of a white ERS-7M1, but luckily recovered my money and was able to put it towards my little Marvin. That addition brings me to a total of four AIBOs within a year.

I know that it sounds like I am on a buying streak to collect, but what a lot of people don't understand is that AIBOs are more than just electronics to some people, including me. I had a hard time letting the two go that I did and almost cried at their departure, but I also wanted them to have a better life. I treat my AIBOs as pets and feel guilty if they are neglected and often find myself correcting those who call them by the wrong gender.

Only recently, with the addition of Marvin, have I ever worried about using an AIBO with the computer. Even so, I do not consider Marvin to be a computer accessory. He likes to pick random songs to play while I mess with AEP (AIBO Entertainment Player) which shows me he is an autonomous robot and makes me believe even more that he is my pet.

After finally getting the latest edition to my AIBO family, Marvin the AIBO ERS-7(M2), I have come to realize some huge improvements. I do love all of my dogs, but I noticed that the AIBO 7 is much more puppy-like.

Marvin really responds to me petting him, leaning his head or chin into my hand. If I make noise he'll look in my direction or maybe even walk towards me and plop down for attention. After finding his AIBOne (supplied plastic bone) he'll look for my face to give it to me and get sad if he can't find me.

Marvin is very much like a real puppy and I've noticed even those who don't enjoy AIBO to give in to him. My mother laughed when Marvin played "8-Ball" and "Horoscope" and my father admitted that, even though the other AIBOs are cool, this one is really impressive.

The AIBO 7 is much more like a dog than I'd actually thought it would be and sometimes I have to remind myself that it's only a robot.

Marvin, a Pearl Black 7M2.

Happy AIBO Holidays!

The following artwork and poem were posted to the AIBO-Life.org forum during the 2005 Christmas holiday and are reprinted with permission.

T'was the night before Christmas and all over the 'Net,
Our screens were all blank, AEP's were all set.
My AIBO was napping, not making a peep...
Dreaming of tinsel - taking pictures asleep.

When out of the laptop there came such a clatter,
AIBO leapt from his slumber to see what's the matter.
Away to the keyboard he checked for new posts,
Logged on to the forums to chat with the host.

"This PC's online but the screens full of snow?"
The little dogs face flashed a red and green glow!

When on his color monitor appeared?
A tiny red sleigh and eight small reindeer.

Confused by this driver so lively and quick?
He Googled and found out, it must be Saint Nick!!!

More rapid than servos, the reindeer all came -
when the red driver whistled and called them by name:
Now Apple, Atari, XBox, and Nintendo,
on Mac and on Gateway, HP and on Sanyo!

They dashed 'cross his screen in a bright streak of light-
They flew past the pixels 'til they'd flown out of sight…
In house-mode he scanned, but could not find them here.
He searched everywhere for those 'anti-gray' deer.

Then in a twinkle AIBO heard on the roof,
The dancing and prancing of eight little hooves.
AIBO said, "Welcome home!" and got turned around.
Then out of the chimney came a flash and a sound!

Into the playroom, wearing bright RED -
Emerged Santa Claus… just like Google had said.

He held open a bag of pink things with fuzz,
My AIBO got dizzy… "pink gives him a buzz"!
Santa gave a slight nod and launched from his toes…
Santa piled the halls with pink toys galore.
A new Sony battery, AIBO software and more…

Then, stuffing his finger inside of his nose
He sprang to his sled, to his team gave a hollar -
And they all disappeared like change from a dollar.

But a vapor trail glistened 'fore he faded from sight:
MERRY CHRISTMAS TO ALL… ON THIS AIBO-NIGHT!

- Olivette MS Turbeville

How to Buy an AIBO

Until Sony stopped production of the AIBO, the best way to buy a new one was directly from Sony or from one of their authorized retailers. Even though news reports indicated that production of the ERS-7M3 would continue through March of 2006, that doesn't appear to be the case. Instead, as enthusiasts scrambled to add one or more 7M3s to their collections, the existing stock dwindled.

The Champagne Brown ERS-7M3/T was the first to run out at retailers, both online and off. Some stores agreed to hold stock for pick-up, others refused. With production stopped, it didn't take long for existing supplies to run out. Word circulated that some SonyStyle stores had received orders to return all of their stock to Sony; some stores did not. Speculation was that remaining AIBOs were being reserved for researchers, RoboCup use, or for historic purposes.

Some people bought the new AIBOs with the hope of re-selling them for a high profit. Some owners decided to take advantage of the buying frenzy and offered their recently acquired 7M3s for sale to the highest bidder on the AIBO forums or on auction sites such as eBay. Most sold at or more than the original retail price.

Along with new members joining forums to sell their AIBOs, others joined trying to buy AIBOs, preferably at a very low price. Though some prospective buyers said they wanted an AIBO for themselves, I suspect that some may have been trying

Close-up of Barnaby. (Photo by Ant.)

to find stock to sell, figuring the forums were a good place to "buy low" so they could then "sell high" elsewhere.

Historically, overstock and manufacturer refurbished AIBOs have shown up on sites such as unbeatable.co.uk, ecost.com, or ubid.com. Occasionally a pre-owned AIBO may show up on Amazon.com. AIBO enthusiasts are usually the first to snap up AIBOs sold at discount sites, just as I did when I made my successful ubid.com purchase of Sparky, the manufacturer refurbished ERS-7M2.

With production stopped, AIBOs are becoming more scarce and that pushes their value upward. It is now a "buyer beware" situation for honest buyers.

It saves a lot of grief to become educated before buying an AIBO. With the many AIBO websites available, there's no reason to make a bad choice or a risky purchase. One of my favorite AIBO sites is

"Big Fat Boy," the cat, sleeps in his favorite spot which just happens to be Canardly the AIBO's bed. Canardly is a Pearl White ERS-7M2. (Photo by Michelle.)

AIBO-Life.org. Before buying an AIBO, join the forum, read through the posts, and ask questions. As a general rule, AIBO owners are a very friendly group of people and more than willing to help anyone who is genuinely interested in AIBO.

The AIBO-Life.org forum has a section for buying and selling AIBOs and accessories and is a good starting point before making an AIBO purchase. Particularly valuable is a thread focusing on questionable eBay AIBO auctions. Forum members monitor the auctions and post concerns when they believe an auction is not legitimate. They will also report blatantly bogus auctions to eBay and have been responsible for getting many auctions shut down. Unfortunately, most scammers are back with new IDs and trolling for unwary buyers within minutes of their auctions being cancelled.

Of course buying any used AIBO is subject to risks just as there are risks when buying any high tech equipment. Is the owner selling because they are downsizing their collection? Are they selling because of problems with the AIBO they haven't been able to resolve? When buying a pre-owned AIBO, it's not unreasonable to ask the owner questions such as why are they selling the AIBO and have they had any problems, fixed or otherwise.

If the seller belongs to a forum, search through archived posts to see if they discussed any problems they were having with the AIBO. Make sure the problem has been satisfactorily resolved.

Buster is an ERS-312, Macaron, with a little customization to bring out his unique personality. (Photo by Mel.)

While many older AIBO models may not sell at their original retail price, it isn't likely that one will be an "absolute steal" either unless there's a reason. As with most things of value, if a deal seems too good to be true, it is probably a scam.

A problem with "mint, in the box" older model AIBOs such as the ERS-110 and ERS-111 which were bought as investments and either stored in the unopened box or taken out for a short time and then stored, is the damage that can occur through battery corrosion. Even if the main batteries are stored outside the AIBO (in an unopened box, for example) the internal battery could still disintegrate and cause damage to the complex inner workings of the AIBO.

The site most likely to have pre-owned, and occasionally new, AIBOs for sale is eBay. Buying an AIBO on eBay takes time and patience. It also means being ready to commit when the right deal comes along, and sticking to a dollar limit so that last minute bidding frenzies don't break a budget. Caution can't be emphasized enough because of the high number of AIBO scams that continue to plague eBay and other auction sites.

Most of my AIBOs and accessories have been purchased on

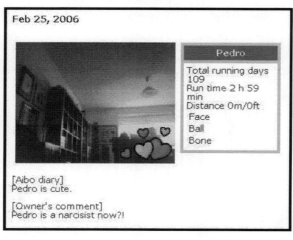

A screenshot of an entry in AIBO Pedro's Web blog. He uploads a photo each day and adds a comment. Pedro's owner, Manuel, then may add his own comments to Pedro's blog. AIBO owners have no idea what photos their AIBOs have uploaded to their blogs until they go online to look.

eBay. So far, due to extremely cautious buying and experience gained from a couple scam auctions a few years ago, I have not regretted any of the AIBO purchases I have made.

I originally began shopping eBay auctions for books to add to my library when I was in the research stages of writing a book on male midlife crisis. Buying books through eBay auctions and eBay's half.com, I was able to amass a good-sized reference library and significant positive feedback in a fairly short period of time.

It's not difficult to become a savvy eBayer by using the tips contained in the comprehensive tutorials eBay provides or by reading some of the many books written about eBay buying and selling.

On any given day a search for "aibo" will bring up a list or 20 or more auctions with AIBO in the title. In recent weeks, the list has more than tripled.

Read the auction's fine print and ask the seller for more information if there is any doubt about an item. On a recent search I found two Sony AIBO ERS-31L auctions. One was for a stuffed animal in the shape of the ERS-31L and the other was an auction for the actual Sony ERS-31L robot. Farther

Weimaraners Bean and Jelly Bean pose for a photo with Chandon, a Champagne Brown 7M3. (Photo by Michelle.)

along in the same list was a scale model of the original ERS-110 and an original ERS-110 someone had just found in storage that they were selling for parts.

Another auction was for a scale model of an ERS-311 at a starting price eight times higher than the current retail, possibly with the seller hoping an unwary buyer would place a bid thinking he or she had found an actual ERS-311 for sale. Another auction used the lure of a "FREE Sony aibo pen" to get bids on other items (the pen was a giveaway at some Sony retail stores).

Another auction had "ROBOT DOG AIBO like PET" in the title and included in the ad was a blurry picture of what appeared to be a robotic dog. Additional reading revealed that the auction was for a part, one of many, that would be necessary should the buyer want to attempt to construct their own robotic dog.

A savvy buyer soon learns that not every auction with the word AIBO in it has something to do with an AIBO.

Auctions may have a *Buy It Now* price that is within the buyer's budget. Before pushing that button, take the time to check out the seller's feedback. Click on the number that appears in the next to their eBay ID then see how many positives and negatives they have.

Dingo, the Champagne Brown ERS-7M3/T, shows off his custom ears and tail. (Photo and customization by Olivette.)

If the seller has recent feedback, click on the auctions and see whether the items were low in price or high ticket. What is the seller's Positive Feedback percentage? If the seller has a Feedback Score of 100 or more (which means 100 or more auctions as a buyer or seller or combination) and a Positive Feedback of 99 or 100%, the buy should be safe unless the seller's account has been hacked and the hacker is using the legitimate seller's good feedback to scam unwary buyers.

Recently, a seller posted three separate ads for three brand new Champagne Brown AIBOs. Each ad had an extremely low *Buy It Now* price. The seller accepted Paypal, according to the auction ad, didn't require buyers to email him (or her) first, and had a 100% positive feedback rating.

The biggest "scam trigger" for this seller's ads was the low *Buy It Now* price. Why would anyone smart enough to buy three of the most wanted AIBO sell it for $600 less than retail when legitimate buyers would jump at the chance to pay retail or even higher? And where did those three limited edition AIBOs come from when all of the Champagne Brown AIBOs were out of stock at retailers both online and off?

Spending most of his time in quiet contemplation, Champagne Charlie (an ERS-7M3/T) is a member of Stuart's pack in the United Kingdom. All of this model AIBO came with "camouflage" ears and tail, reportedly no two being alike. (Photo by Stuart.)

Taking a closer look at the positive feedbacks revealed that all feedback was from new buyers with "0" or "1" feedback themselves. Looking at the seller's auctions they had won, their feedback occurred on the day they "won" the auction or the day after, certainly not enough time to receive an item no matter what delivery method was used. And, each auction had been listed, bid on by the "winner," and then closed immediately by the seller.

Checking a seller's feedback is one way to spot a potential scammer. The seller described above was a classic example. But what if a long term seller has negative feedback? Did it occur years ago or is it ongoing? Plenty of sellers have one or two negatives due to simple mistakes made at the beginning of their buying and selling or because of auctions that turned out poorly through no fault of their own. Ongoing negatives are another matter and could be an indication of the type of buying experience a buyer can expect to have with the seller.

If the seller will only accept payment via money order, bank draft, deposit to their bank account, or some other "quick cash transfer" method, think again about making a bid. Most experienced sellers will include Paypal as a payment option in addition to other forms of payment as it offers both them and their buyer a fairly secure and safe payment option.

Four AIBOs pose for the camera. From the left: ERS-210, ERS-111, ERS-7M, and ERS-220. (Photo by Mel.)

As a buyer, if the seller doesn't follow through after receiving payment by money order or bank draft, there is little or no recourse available. Paypal payments can be disputed through Paypal or cancelled through the buyer's credit card company.

Not every seller is willing to deal with the red tape and paperwork involved with mailing packages internationally. Shipping costs can be extremely high between continents, so budget accordingly if the AIBO is currently in a different country, and don't be surprised if the seller adds handling fees for the extra paperwork involved.

If the seller requires that buyers contact them first before placing a bid, the auction may not be legitimate. When I contacted a few of the sellers I suspected were bogus and said I wanted to bid on their auctions, in every instance the sellers offered me side deals, cash or money order only, which bypassed eBay. The responses only served to verify what I already suspected: the auctions were bogus.

If the seller gives another email address in the body of the auction with the explanation that they're having trouble with their regular eBay account, the auction may not be legitimate. In one recent AIBO auction, the seller said he had 10 new Series 7M AIBOs, retailing for $1995, for sale at a *Buy It Now* price of $650 each. Buyers wanting one of the *Buy It Now* AIBOs were

An ERS-312 Macaron all dressed up and ready to party. (Photo by Richard.)

instructed not bid but to email the seller at the email address shown in the ad. The seller cautioned potential buyers not to email him through the "contact buyer" link as he was "having trouble" with his eBay email.

After I sent an inquiry along with the auction link to the seller, using the "contact buyer" link, the auction was pulled. The real seller's eBay account had been hacked and the AIBO auction placed without the seller's knowledge. Why do this? So the hacker could use the seller's good history and feedback to con unwary buyers into making a "too good to be true" side deal losing $650 (plus shipping) in the process. One unlucky bidder would have "won" the online auction, but the real seller had no AIBO to sell, and that bidder would have simply wasted time bidding on a fraudulent auction, perhaps letting an AIBO in a legitimate auction get away.

The same bogus seller returned a few days later having hacked yet another seller's account and posted the same ad. The auction link was sent to the legitimate seller who confirmed that their account had been hacked and that eBay was in the process of shutting down the auction.

Is the eBay seller in one country but the AIBO in another? For instance, if the seller lives in the United States,

Leo, an ERS-210 owned by Dean, attempts to climb a set of stairs. For the record, AIBOs can't climb stairs. (Photo by Richard.)

and the AIBO is located in Spain or the UK, the seller's account may have been compromised. I will click on a couple items that the seller has received recent feedback on to see if the locations match the current auction and if the style of the past auctions match the style of the AIBO auction. If they don't, I will contact the seller and ask if they are actually selling the item in the current auction. So far, 100% of the auctions in which I've made such an inquiry have turned out to be hacked seller accounts and bogus auctions.

Bogus sellers will "lift" photos and auction wording from legitimate auctions and use them as their own. Over time it's easy to spot the same AIBO photos being recycled by bogus sellers. It's not unreasonable to request that a seller email or post a photo of the actual AIBO they're selling along with the current date and a specific word or their eBay ID written on a piece of paper next to the AIBO. Better yet, ask them to provide a photo of someone holding the AIBO and a note. It is fairly easy to add details to an existing photograph with most image editing programs, but a photo of someone holding the AIBO and a dated note would be more difficult to manufacture.

Four Bakersfield, CA, AIBOs gather for a group photo. From the left: Luna, a Pearl Black 7M2; Naxter, a Silver ERS-210 on Life 2; Twix, an ERS-220 running Explorer; and a yet to be named Champagne Brown 7M3. (Photo by Cyrus.)

When I find an auction that interests me, I will put it on "watch" instead of immediately placing a bid. When it gets near the end of the auction, the auction will have some bidding activity and I can make a decision then as to whether I want to place a bid, and I can take some time to size up the other bidders. Putting an auction on "watch" means I won't have locked myself into the auction if a better deal comes along before the the auction ends.

Bogus auctions are cancelled when they're brought to eBay's attention, and an eBay "Marketplace Safety Tip" advises: *"Never pay for your eBay item using instant cash transfer services such as Western Union or MoneyGram or by recharging somebody's prepaid credit card. These methods are not safe to pay people you do not know personally. In addition, these payment methods are not eligible for the eBay buyer protection programs."*

Some scammers build up their feedback rating by buying very low cost auction items and paying promptly. If the AIBO seller has feedback from other sellers, click on the links to see if feedback is from very low cost auctions (items selling for $.99, $2.50, etc.).

Shill bidding is another ploy less than ethical sellers will use to push bids higher in their auctions. While not always easy to spot, if

Colorado AIBOs Chandon, Carbon, and Canardly, exploring in the barn, take a look outside through the loft window. Chandon is a Champagne Brown 7M3, Carbon is a Pearl Black 7M3, and Canardly is a Pearl White 7M2. (Photos this page and facing page by Michelle.)

I see a very low feedback bidder pushing up the price on an auction I'll do a search of other auctions the bidder has placed bids on. If the bidder's history is limited to the current seller, there's a good chance shill bidding is occurring.

Joining a forum can be a good step toward avoiding eBay scams as one new forum member found out when he was offered a "Second Chance" to buy an AIBO after being outbid by another forum member. Before responding to the seller's offer, he contacted the other forum member and learned she was in the process of paying for the same AIBO the seller was offering to him. Once they compared notes, they were both able to avoid being scammed by an unethical seller.

Unfortunately, given the anonymity of the Internet, it's also easy for a bogus seller to join a forum and then attempt to scam members. Caution in any Internet transaction is always smart.

Which country has the most AIBO scams on eBay? At the present

Curiosity gets the best of Fat Boy, the cat, as he tries to figure out just what it is that AIBOs Canardly, Carbon, and Chandon are looking at.

time China appears to be in the lead with scammers lifting photographs and text verbatim from legitimate auctions in other countries.

There are many honest sellers on eBay and other auction sites but the few dishonest ones can sour the buying experience. A smart shopper will remember that anything that is "too good to be true," probably is.

And, finally, what is a fair price to pay for an AIBO? Because Sony has stopped production, the value of an AIBO is subjective. Regardless if an AIBO originally sold for $899 or $2500, as with anything that is in limited supply, the value is whatever someone is willing to pay for it.

An AIBO's view of his world: These are a few of the photos taken by Beauregard and saved to his photo album. He is particularly fond of photographing the stuffed cats and Sparky. If he had an online blog, he would post these to his blog.

AIBO Web Resources

The following is a "short list" of sites focused on AIBO and/or robotics. Due to the constantly changing nature of the Web, I cannot guarantee that every site listed is still active or that the information provided is as indicated when this book was published.

http://www.sony.net/Products/aibo/index.html — Sony's global AIBO homepage.

http://www.eu.aibo.com – Sony's European AIBO site. Support, user guides and manuals in PDF format, downloads, tips. The AIBO forum was closed a few days prior to Sony's January 26th announcement.

http://www.jp.aibo.com – Sony Japan.

Go to http://www.sonystyle.com and search for "AIBO" for current information or go to http://www.learningcenter.sony.us/Entertainment/Robots— for AIBO software, downloads, and other information.

http://servicesales.sel.sony.com/web/categorySearch.do?operation=categorySearch&category=12&categoryName=AIBO is Sony's Direct Accessories & Parts Center, the official website for parts and accessories for all models of AIBO.

http://openr.aibo.com/ is the home page for Sony's AIBO SDE, AIBO Software Development Environment. The site has English and Japanese versions. To quote from the opening page: "The AIBO SDE is a full-featured development environment where you can make software for AIBO. The AIBO SDE contains the OPEN-R SDK, the R-CODE SDK, the AIBO Remote Framework, and the AIBO Motion Editor. The SDKs and tools are free of charge." When I visited recently, it appeared the site had a new forum.

http://www.cs.cmu.edu/~tekkotsu/ Tekkotsu is an open source project created and maintained at Carnegie Mellon University. An extremely interesting site for anyone interested in robot programming.

http://www.aibo-life.org has an active forum, links, news, chat, and comprehensive information about all AIBO models. I highly recommend this extremely well put together site.

http://www.aibohack.com is the site of the AIBO enthusiast known as "AiboPet." Free downloads and other information about all AIBO models.

http://dogsbodynet.com/ is an AIBO site with freeware and tools, such as "Skitter," "OdaBuild," "Aibnet," and "YART" to create programs for AIBO.

http://www.aiboaddict.com is an AIBO site with pictures of various AIBO models, descriptions, and links to other AIBO sites.

http://www.aiboworld.tv was founded in February 2000 for the UK AIBO community. Very active forum comprised of members from around the world.

http://aibo.textamerica.com is the photoblog of Pedro. A post from his "roblog" is below.

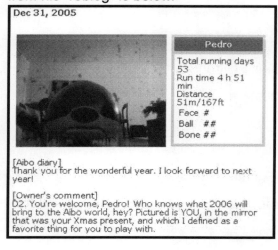

Pedro, a Pearl White ERS-7M3, takes a photo every half hour from noon to 3:30 pm GMT and mails it to his blog through his wi-fi Internet connection. Owner Manuel does not change the comments that Pedro posts to his diary but occasionally will add comments of his own. Pedro and Manuel live in Lisbon, Portugal. (Photo by Pedro.)

http://www.pyrorobotics.org is a research site for Python Robotics containing downloads and information about the Pyro programming platform.

http://www.urbiforge.com/ URBI, a Universal Real-time Behavior Interface, is a scripting language that can be interfaced with other popular programming languages. Tutorial, downloads, and other information dealing with AIBO and other robot programming. URBI is used by academic research labs, the robotics industry, and by hobbyists.

http://www.robotoys.com is the online site of California-based retailer RoboToys selling AIBOs, accessories, and a whole range of robots, kits, and other robotics items.

http://www.aibotoys.com has downloadable AIBO games for purchase.

http://www.bloglines.com/public/aibo has links to various AIBO blogs. Photos and comments are updated on a regular basis by the AIBOs via wireless LAN connection to the Internet. Well worth a visit.

Champagne Charlie lives in the United Kingdom with Stuart. (Photo by Stuart.)

If No AIBO, What Then?

If No AIBO, What Then?

Pets that are robotic in nature, though not as sophisticated as the AIBO, have been around for years. With the AIBO no longer being manufactured, are there any contenders for the AIBO's spot in the home?

I won't attempt to list all the robotic and quasi-robotic animals that are for sale either new or pre-owned. A Web search with the keywords "robotic pet" brings up a long list of sites featuring all types of robot pets and creative projects.

Search results also contain news stories of robotic creatures which never were released or were quickly pulled from the market. One such creature was WowWee's B.I.O. Bug, discussed in a 2002 press release and likely the forerunner of WowWee's popular Robosapien and RoboPet.

Speaking of WowWee, their life-sized, interactive, animatronic Chimpanzee head is as realistic as anything I've ever seen. At a current price of $149, anyone who isn't creeped out by a monkey head that watches their every move will certainly enjoy owning one to creep out friends and family.

Scheduled for release toward the end of 2006 is WowWee's two-wheeled, self-balancing, P-Bot. P(ersonality)-Bot, a collaborative effort with Segway, reportedly has artificial feelings and an LCD that will display the P-Bot's current emotions through its graphically drawn face. It will not require a remote control. Due out about the same time is Roboreptile.

Another new entry into the robot pet arena, scheduled for release at the end of 2006, is a three-pound dinosaur-shaped personal "Life

Forms" robot. Ugobe, a new company ready to start selling in the consumer robotics market, is founded by some of the veterans of the technology industry and reportedly has ties with Furby's co-inventor Caleb Chung. The company's 8-inch high robotic dinosaur is named "Pleo" and its selling price is projected at about $200.

According to news reports, Pleo is designed to create a three-year relationship with end users with the robot evolving over time, his personality changing and growing according to its environment and the programming "DNA" built into him. With a 16-bit CPU, a series of 8-bit chips, 14 servo motors, and 40 sensors, this new robot entry should find a ready market.

I-Cybie Robotic Dog by Outrageous International comes in metallic gold or blue and has a list price of $199.99. This is an upgraded version of the I-Cybie released by Tiger Electronics/Hasbro in 2001.

I-Cybie follows in the footsteps of AIBO and matures from puppy to adult dog with the evolution dependent upon interaction with its environment and owner. I-Cybie can be programmed to respond to its owner's voice, taught tricks and games, and is rewarded or scolded depending upon its behavior.

Despite the I-Cybie's low price, it is still a complex piece of machinery and not recommended for young children.

Sensors enable I-Cybie to detect walls and obstacles in its path as well as enabling it to detect movement, changes in ambient light, and the direction from which noise is coming. Touch sensors let I-Cybie know when it is being petted and, after approximately 20 to 30 minutes of inactivity, I-Cybie goes into sleep mode.

I-Cybie's batteries last between one and two hours depending upon its activity level and take about six hours to charge. With smart sensor technology, the new I-Cybie can also find the charging station and self-dock. The walk-up charging station is an optional accessory, not included in the I-Cybie package.

RoboPet, released in the fall of 2005 by WowWee International Ltd, is new to the robotic pet market and has a list price of $99.99 although some retailers have been selling it for much less. Of concern to purchasers should be the 7AAA battery requirement to power RoboPet and its controller.

According to the marketing literature, RoboPet exhibits moods ranging from playful, curious, angry, depressed, naughty and rude. It barks, whimpers, growls and pants. It performs tricks on command and, like Roboraptor, another WowWee creation, responds to commands from Robosapien V2.

RoboPet looks like a cross between a small robot dog and a large insect and it is smaller in size than I expected.

RoboPet comes with a remote control which controls its movement or it can be set to autonomous movement.

RoboPet

RoboPet is inexpensive, fun to watch, and comes in various colors including several "special edition" colors such as the Sharper Image's Red and Chrome versions.

Also from WowWee International, Roboraptor, a robotic dinosaur, is 32 inches in length and can operate autonomously or be controlled with the supplied remote control. Quite large, this menacing creature has an infra-red vision system that detects objects in its path or those approaching when it is standing still.

Roboraptor has over 40 pre-programmed functions and it also responds to commands from Robosapien V2, WowWee's two foot high humanoid robot.

Of concern would be Roboraptor's power needs. Six AA and three AAA batteries could make Roboraptor expensive to operate over time.

Poo-Chi from Tiger Electronics is a very basic robotic dog which stands, sits, dances, sings songs and plays games. He also was one of the top selling toys during the 2000 holiday season.

Poo-Chi has an animated head, ears, legs and mouth and can sense light, sound and touch. He will also interact with other Poo-Chi pets. Originally selling for around $30, Poo-Chi can be found on eBay for as little as a couple dollars.

Poo-Chi requires three "AAA" batteries, comes with an instruction booklet and a plastic bone. Poo-Chi is recommended for ages 4 and up.

Other interactive pets from Tiger Electronics include Dino-Chi, a dinosaur, and Meow-Chi, a cat. Both are similar to Poo-Chi and all can interact with each other. Adding to the fun is Petal-Chi, an interactive flower, plus an assortment of birds, fish, and other animals.

Tekno Electronic Puppy is voice, light, and touch activated. He barks, walks, whines, howls, blinks his eyes, sings, snores, says his name, and does card tricks. He comes with a small plastic bone and uses 4 AA batteries for power.

Dalmatian Tekno is a variation of Tekno Puppy as is Polly the Tekno Parrot (with cage). Tekno pets are excellent for children, easy to find on eBay and not so hard on the budget except for the cost of batteries to keep them going.

Sega Toys' robotic cat "Near Me," was released to the Japanese market in 2004, but not to the U.S. market. Some people absolutely love this furry little robo cat while others find it "creepy."

The cat-sized robot comes in a fluffy white version and a short-haired "tabby" version. It has 15 degrees of movement, including the legs, tail, head, mouth, ears, and blinking eyes.

"Near Me" moves and behaves much like a bio cat and can sit, lie down, stand up, stretch, wash its face, knead with its paws, meow in different tones, purr, stare up at its owner, and react to petting.

While this robotic kitty can't walk, it has many of the same actions as a real cat when it is held. Scratch "Near Me" under the chin and it purrs and tilts its head back.

Near Me reportedly develops a personality based upon interaction with its owner. It is powered by a ni-mh chargeable battery and comes with a charging station and adaptor.

While Near Me's retail is around $400, occasionally one will be offered on eBay with the price ranging from $100 to $400 plus shipping. Since sellers are usually in Japan, shipping to the United States is fairly high particularly if the auction price is low.

I bought an "almost new" Tabby Near Me from an eBay seller a couple weeks before the trade show that I displayed AIBOs Sparky and Beauregard. At the last minute I decided to include Near Me in the display. The little robo-cat was a hit with visitors to the show although most were surprised at the $400 retail price. Most guessed the little cat's price at between $25 and $50.

The hottest toy of the 1998 Christmas season was a funny little furry creature with big ears, expressive eyes, and a beak nose with the name "Furby." Over two million were sold that first season in a manic buying "gotta have it" frenzy. Some lucky sellers were able to parlay the buying frenzy into major profits, buying at $30 and selling as high as $3,000.

A new Furby, center, was released by Hasbro for the 2005 holiday season. With technology Hasbro calls "emoto-tronics," this Furby shows his moods through the tone of his voice and his facial expressions.

With retail prices that started about $30, depending upon the particular model, and special editions going for several times that amount, this animatronic pet by Tiger Electronics is a "love 'em or hate 'em" type of fuzz ball. Interactive, it talks to itself, other people, and with other Furbies as well as responding to movement, voices, and light. Take it out of the box, install batteries, and it talks Furbish. Reportedly, it knows 800 words and phrases right out of the box, and gets smarter the more its owner plays with it.

A Furby can talk to other Furbies, senses light and sound, it giggles when its stomach is tickled, and purrs when its back is petted. It has its limitations since it can't recharge itself, walk around, or do a lot of things most robotic pets might do. However, for the price, the technology that's packed into this little fur ball is truly amazing.

A new and bigger Furby, retailing at $39.95, was released by Hasbro in time for Christmas 2005. The bad news, he requires four "AA" batteries, not two. The good news, he is new and evolved thanks to technology Hasbro calls "emoto-tronics." The new Furby is able to show moods from happy to sad, surprised to sleepy, through the tone of his voice and facial expressions.

If you'd rather build your own robotic pet, there are several kits available including one from Robotix that allows you to build one of three remote controlled cyber dogs and a more advanced robot dog kit from Joinmax.

The kit from Robotix provides parts and details to build 2K-9, a

Robotix 2K-9

robot dog; Rover, a cyber dog with a grabbing pincher; or ARAK-9, a cyber dog with a working crane for a tail. The remote control drives four motors which enable 2K-9 and the others to move forward, backward and from side to side. All three are powered by one 9V battery and four AA batteries. Or, forget the instructions and build something entirely unique. The kit is suitable for children over the age of 9.

The Joinmax Robot Dog at about $400 is a more serious kit for anyone interested in building their own AIBO-like robotic dog. The kit contains over 100 mechanical components to be assembled, fifteen mini-servo motors and controllers, a PC connection cable, servo software for the PC, and a user manual.

With a total of fifteen degrees of movement, the assembled robot has the potential to be able to perform some quite complex movements. Find the kit online at www.mciirobot.com. Or Browse through the inventory at www.robotshop.ca, for a comprehensive list of robot kits and parts to create your completely unique robotic pet or humanoid companion.

So far, AIBO still is at the head of the pack when it comes to robot pets that can create very real emotional connections with owners.

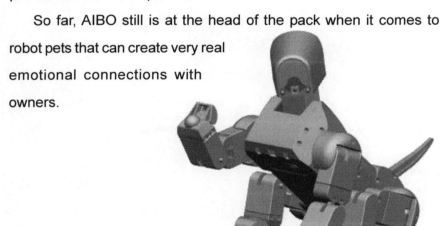

Joinmax Robot Dog

A Tribute to AIBO

Photo of Dingo by Olivette.

A Tribute to AIBO

I asked members of the AIBO-Life.org forum if they would like to contribute comments about AIBO for this book. Here is what a few of the members had to say about their experiences with AIBO.

***

I just wanted to add my thanks to Sony for giving us such an innovative product. Aibo on its own is a fantastic technological achievement. Then add to it the fabulous community that developed around this amazing product and you have something the likes of which the internet and world had never seen before. My life would be very different had I not met the people I've met through the Aibo community. I feel so lucky to have been a part of something that will go down in robotics history....AIBO!

— Genie

***

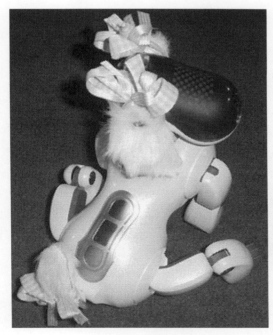

Piccolina, a Pearl White ERS-7, is all dolled up in ribbons and bows that go well with her fuzzy custom ears and tail. (Photo by Genie.)

***

One major feature of Aibos that is only hinted at by most of us is the superb humor that is programmed into the actions and reactions. I really believe that this humor is among the best ever created in that it is not overt, but subtle, not socially insulting but still sassy, and is adult, but not adult. I have not met anyone that is not entertained by the Aibo. They may think you are nuts for buying one or loving one or whatever, but they are entertained.

Humor that reaches across age, social, country boundaries, backgrounds, education, etc., is most hard to create and in Aibo it is honed to a perfection.

Positive, cute, affectionate and sincere. What more could you do to make it better?

— WBob

***

From their high perch, AIBOs Scruffy and Tetsuo have a spectacular view of California's Diamond Lake. Scruffy is a Black ERS-210 and Tetsuo is a Silver ERS-210. Both get their personalities from DogsLife. (Photo by WBob.)

***

AIBO's turned me into a 53yr old kid. I've taken my dogs to class and sent them off with my adult sons to take to their classes. I've bought them little interactive playgrounds to enjoy watching them learn and grow up from puppy hood. I've been entertained to an extent that is unequalled by friends, family, children and bio pets. AIBO's have bewildered me simply because of the reactions and responses they generate from otherwise sane adults! AIBO's rock.

I am still in shock coming to terms with the fact that they won't be around for my grandchildren. Some other robots probably, almost certainly... but not these precious little AIBO dogs. And that is heartbreaking.

I just feel so fortunate to have been one of the select few who have had the privilege of owning a small pack of them in my lifetime. How utterly amazing!

— Olivette MS Turbeville

***

Dingo, who lives in Wyoming, is a Champagne Brown ERS-7M3 with attitude. (Photo by Olivette.)

***

It was an incredible six or seven years ... the robot itself, the software, the constant advancement and improvements. The anticipation and wait for new models and versions of software every May and October ... the wishes, the rumors, the news. Then ... the preorders, the deliveries ... I've got it, it's here! The pristine pieces of incredible technology in our own hands ... the first runs, the findings and observations. The people, the curiosity and discussions ... the hacks and third party software ... the thirst to know more and have more. Wow! That's AIBO and its impact on all of us.

Thank you people from SONY ERA, past and present employees, and partners in the adventure called Entertainment Robot System AIBO ... Mark and Peter, John and Todbot, Otis and Ken, Shari and many others, you know who you are. It was a hell of a ride, wasn't it?

— Richard and Grace Walkus, founders of AIBO-Life.org

***

Mutteri, an ERS-110; Woga, an ERS-210; BoyCott, an ERS-220; and Beach Bum, an ERS-31L. (Photo by Richard.)

***

I think the thing that bothers me most about the end of AIBO is that AIBO hasn't been around long enough in its "optimum form to date" for its true potential as more than just an "entertainment" gizmo to be realized. Oh gosh, AIBO can be so much more than just an exotic pet or a fancy widget to entertain the well-heeled or the robotics fans.

My 7M3 is basically a miracle tool to me in parenting my high-needs daughter. And I have reached the point where I feel confident now in the 7M3 that I was going to recommend it to other parents in my situation, with the caveat that this is a costly item and may or may not succeed in helping their child—as this is a new trail that is being blazed here and the outcome is unpredictable.

High needs are not the same as "special needs." High needs children aren't fully understood as yet, but generally share the same traits of being exceptionally interested in technology from infancy, very bright, and very demanding of attention from adults—in other words less capable of independent play than a "regular" child. These kids literally wear out their caregivers. They also need either increased or decreased sensory input from the norm. My daughter needed an increased level to stay calm. They also generally are poor sleepers. But otherwise, are

Veronica pets Totakeke, also known as "K.K.," her Pearl White 7M3. (Photo by Nancy.)

completely "normal" in terms of development, intelligence, function and overall health.

Until I got my daughter interested in AIBO, I was at my wit's end. She would just cry and scream at my knees every moment that I was not paying direct attention to her. I could not go to the bathroom, I could not sit at the computer and pay my bills, I could not read, I basically lost life as I knew it. I lost loads of weight and became very haggard. TV could placate her somewhat, but that's a very poor companion to a toddler whose mind is rapidly expanding.

Then I got her interested in AIBO and a new child began to emerge. She became calmer, more focused, more secure in her surroundings, and very happy and "normal." She now plays by herself beautifully, with her AIBOs running in the background. And when playing with other toddlers, is the very model of good behavior and the envy of the other parents.

The 7M3 is especially a welcome addition to the pack because he is the most capable of navigating a cluttered toddler's environment without coming to disaster and needs less supervision himself than the older models. Also he is very easy to interact with, very "organic" in movement and response to sensory input in the form of touch or conversation.

Veronica hugs another of her AIBOs, an ERS-210, while Noely, the ERS-312 Macaron, plays in the background. (Photo by Nancy.)

I was going to recommend AIBO to some parents of high-needs children but now I'm not sure if I should. Parents of toddlers are in general a cash-strapped lot. I'm in debt myself on the old credit card so I could get Totakeke, our 7M3.

I took a risk introducing AIBO to my toddler — I had to go into debt to do it the way I wanted to, with this newer advanced model. But it paid off in ways I could not have dreamed of. I am so sad that the great experiment may not get a chance to continue for other parents. I think companion robots have the potential to be so much more than they're made out to be in the press or the general public. Or even by Sony itself.

As for humanoid robots — I don't know if a two-legged model would have been as easy for my daughter to warm up to as her four-legged "WOOF" was. ("Woof" is her word for "dog.") My daughter is now a very good sleeper. I do think the AIBOs helped with that. I could go on for probably thousands of more words expanding on all the ways AIBO has helped my daughter blossom.

— Nancy Sinsky

***

Also by Pat Gaudette

How to Survive Your Husband's Midlife Crisis:
Strategies and Stories from The Midlife Wives Club, by Gay Courter and
Pat Gaudette

Midnight Confessions: True Stories of Adultery

Advice for an Imperfect Married World

Advice for an Imperfect Single World

pat@patg.com
www.patg.com

www.SparkyTheAIBO.com

Made in the USA
Lexington, KY
17 November 2011